MW00931588

NARCISSISTIC MOTHERS

HOW TO IDENTIFY HER MANIPULATIVE BEHAVIOURS AND FINALLY DISCOVER YOUR INNER PEACE

LILIA JOHNES

Copyright © 2023. All rights reserved.

The content contained within this book may not be reproduced, duplicated, or transmitted without direct written permission from the author or the publisher.

Under no circumstances will any blame or legal responsibility be held against the publisher or author for any damages, reparation, or monetary loss due to the information contained within this book, either directly or indirectly.

Legal Notice:

This book is copyright protected. It is only for personal use. You cannot amend, distribute, sell, use, quote or paraphrase any part, or the content within this book, without the consent of the author or publisher.

Disclaimer Notice:

Please note the information contained within this document is for educational and entertainment purposes only. All effort has been executed to present accurate, up-to-date, reliable, and complete information. No warranties of any kind are declared or implied. Readers acknowledge that the author is not engaged in the rendering of legal, financial, medical, or professional advice. The content within this book has been derived from various sources. Please consult a licensed professional before attempting any techniques outlined in this book.

By reading this document, the reader agrees that under no circumstances is the author responsible for any losses, direct or indirect, that are incurred as a result of the use of the information contained within this document, including, but not limited to, errors, omissions, or inaccuracies.

CONTENTS

Trigger warning: This book may elicit feelings of past trauma.

INTRODUCTION

Maybe it's generational trauma. Maybe everything she hates about herself, she saw staring back at her through eyes that mirrored her own, a face shaped like hers, hair that fell in the exact same awkward way that hers did. But was that my fault? Was I to be the object of the self-hatred that burned within her? Was I to be the physical representation of all the bad that she painfully clung to, while she only attributed the good to herself? Some children are the objects of their parent's pride. I, on the other hand, was the object of my parent's disdain, trapped in a generational cycle of never escaping.

A BROKEN-HEARTED CHILD—PAIN FROM A MOTHER

My alarm wakes me up as it does every other day, but today it goes off an hour later, which means it's Sunday. But today is different. When I open my eyes and adjust to the bits of sunlight streaming into my room from above the curtain, I take my phone and I am met with a message from my best friend.

Jennifer: Brace yourself... It's Mother's Day!

The realization dawns on me and the response is immediate: the anxiety grips my chest and my heart starts pounding. I try distracting myself by scrolling through social media, but I am met with an onslaught of candid photos of people with their mothers, #appreciationposts for all the moms who are just so great, and an endless number of ads encouraging me to start shopping and buy my own mom a gift that is worthy of a queen. The cynic in me snorts derisively at the posts, wondering why they don't post about their moms every other day if they were, in fact, so great.

The intrusive thoughts fill my mind: *If my mom were as great as you all think your moms are, I would be #appreciationpost-ing her all day, every day.* But that is not the hand I was dealt.

I brush the thought from my mind and make a conscious effort to actively avoid and boycott social media for the rest of the day. This is a reality check for me; it is too much to bear, and it is torture! This torture has cost me ten years of continuous arguments and three years of therapy, all of which have led me here, to writing this book.

There are many anecdotes that I can use to describe my childhood, such as the notion that if you speak positive words to your plant it will grow and flourish, and I can point out the fact that I was always the shortest of all my friends. Or I could talk about how, no matter what I did, including establishing my own successful business, I was just never good enough.

I know that is a pretty heavy introduction, but that is what I faced daily until I found a way of cutting the strings that tethered me to the heartbreak caused by the one person who was meant to protect me and nurture me. My name is Lilia Johnes and, according to my psychologist, I am the victim of psychological abuse from my mother who, in her expert opinion, is a narcissist.

When I realized this, I was shocked. Like many people, I was of the old-school belief that abuse, if not physical, is not real. But let me tell you that, sometimes, emotional scars run deeper than physical ones. By all accounts, people considered me to have led a healthy, happy, and successful life. Growing up in a family of four children, we were lucky enough to never lack for anything. I went to the best schools, attended prestigious universities, and I have worked in several successful roles at reputable consulting firms since my graduation. At 29—what many would consider a young age—I established my own successful business venture.

If I were anyone else, I would have been proud of myself. But from my mother's perspective, nothing I did was ever enough.

Now, I know this seems like a lot to take in; we're only just getting acquainted and I am pouring out my heart and soul to you. But there is a reason you're here, reading this book.

I decided to write this book as someone who understands the pains of being raised by a mother who doesn't appreciate you, or who maybe doesn't know how to appreciate you. You may find yourself in the uniquely difficult position of being torn between loving the woman who gave you life and hating her for emotionally abusing you when you were growing up. Maybe you are tired of the abuse, or maybe, for the longest time, you didn't even know that you were facing emotional and psychological abuse, but you suffer from inexplicable trauma that you suspect originates from your mother. Maybe you have struggled in finding true love because your relationships are built on a foundation of fear, distrust, and trauma, which is something that may have originated from your childhood trauma. Maybe you just need help to find ways of healing from the scars that have been so deeply embedded in your heart and mind.

Well, I have once been in this exact same position. But I am here to help you find balance in loving someone who is often difficult to love; I am here to help you identify the narcissistic behaviors and find the healing at the end of the tunnel; I am here to help you identify toxic cycles and escape those cycles; and I am here to provide you with tried and tested strategies to heal from the trauma.

By the end of this book, you will have gone through the steps that are necessary to heal yourself and find true happiness. You will no longer be enslaved by what happened in your childhood and adulthood, and you will find ways of treating the pain and coping with your mother.

The reality that has quickly dawned on me is that I wasn't the only one who faced this emotional and psychological abuse. Granted, I only noticed how strange my relationship with my mother was when I saw others with their mothers. I only realized what I *didn't* have when I saw what others *did* have.

There are men and women from all walks of life—who are either single or married with kids, who are financially stable or just managing to make ends meet, who face unseen challenges on a daily basis—that are deeply rooted in pain caused by the one person that was supposed to protect them from pain.

There are also those people who manage to find a person that they can love. They manage to settle down and grow their families, but sometimes they feel like they are unable to give the best versions of themselves to their families. Sometimes, all they can do is hope to not have any mental breakdowns when they are with their family. Others may find themselves actively choosing not to be like their mothers when they are raising their own kids, but this often leads to them overcorrecting or overcompensating in the opposite direction.

I hope this book will bring hope to the broken-hearted adults who are victims of narcissistic mothers. I hope that my words will serve as a tool to empower them and transform their lives while soothing the wounds that are so deeply entrenched in their hearts.

Let us go on the journey to find the balance between loving your mother while taking care of your own mental health. After all, you can't throw away the person who has birthed you and raised you.

1

THE "MOTHER" WOUND

How can you identify the root cause of your trauma and pain when you don't even know that you have experienced trauma and pain? To identify the root, you must first identify the problem, and to do that, you need a baseline from which to work.

Have you ever been told that "good girls" behave in a particular way? Have you ever had the whole version of who you are compressed and shoved into a small box so that you neatly fit into what the world deems appropriate for women and girls? Or have you found yourself facing unrealistic expectations and trying to live up to what is expected of a "real man"?

This is a warped sense of what the person we love the most has allowed us to think for most of our lives.

Who is your first love? I ask you this because more often than not, our minds tend to think of our first romantic love. But, even before we understand the concept of romantic love, we experience one of the most natural forms of love to ever exist: the love of a mother.

The relationship and bond between a mother and child are absolutely extraordinary and profound. They form the foundation upon which all other relationships in our lives will be based. Whether directly or indirectly, we learn how to love and how to be loved by this dominating maternal force in our lives, and whether or not this love is deemed correct or incorrect is often indiscernible.

Our mothers are meant to love us and keep us safe.

But, as much as our mothers are the source of light in our lives, their role is far more complex. As we grow from children into adults, we question our mothers' actions and we wonder why they raised us the way we did. We think that their sole role was to mother us as children.

This false conception of mothers being just mothers is a flawed understanding created in this "man's world" that we live in. What makes this false understanding even worse is that women believe these misconceptions about themselves and pass these false beliefs onto their daughters, trying to neatly fit them into the boxes that misogynistic cultures have created. But the world no longer works this way, and these beliefs that have been ingrained in women's minds from previous generations no longer fit into a world where women are easily allowed and encouraged to take up space. With these unrealistic weights and expectations passed down from generation to generation, women are faced with a unique challenge and difficulty that impacts their most fundamental relationship: the mother-child relationship (Nguyen, 2021).

THE MOTHER WOUND

When a woman is led to believe that she is unworthy or even inferior to men, she may do one of two things. Either she will succumb to the belief, or she will fight this belief with everything in her. In many instances, if a woman chooses to fight this belief, these differing beliefs will find themselves fighting against each other as it is a mother and a daughter in the same home trying to fulfill very different roles in society.

You see, in past generations—the generations of our mothers and grandmothers—women were taught to be subservient to men. They were taught that good girls are inferior to men and that they need to cater to a man's needs, usually to the detriment of their own self-worth and independence. Women were taught to give up their wants and needs, or to place themselves and what they value on the backburner as a way of giving the best to those around them.

Unfortunately, the people who taught women to do this were, in fact, also women, who were taught the exact same thing by the generation that came before them. And this "generational trauma" continued (Nguyen, 2021). The fact that women were teaching their daughters to fit into a box didn't mean that they agreed with the concept, and this is often where the trauma began.

It is here that we see the detrimental effects of self-sacrifice. These constraints are passed down from generation to generation with the false idealization that "women are meant to be in the kitchen," if you will.

Constantly doing and putting others before themselves in the name of being a good woman, and teaching their daughters to do the same even though they know how draining and exhausting it is, may be a weight that is often too heavy for their shoulders. And this weight is passed on to little girls whose shoulders are not strong enough.

But the path that leads to the mother wound doesn't start and end with little girls, and men can even face this too. In fact, while the patriarchy is most often seen to affect women, women of color, and those of strained financial circumstances, men can also experience the mother wound by continuing this "expected behavior" of women in their lives, i.e., keeping the patriarchy going.

The Role of a Mother

If you have found yourself, as an individual, always lacking—whether in love, intimacy, security, or anything else—you may have found yourself wondering what you have done in life to always get the short end of the stick. But when the benchmark for love and affection, and all the things you *need* has been set so low, it makes affording yourself the opportunity of happiness quite rare.

There are basic things that you need from your parents to survive. Food, clothes, warmth, and a roof over your head are the basic needs that any child has for survival. And while it is easy to fulfill these needs and keep a human alive, their needs go so much deeper than that.

We are complex beings, and survival mode is not the condition we are meant to constantly live in. Our needs go far deeper than having just food and clothes, but when this is all a child ever receives, having any greater expectations may seem like you're asking for too much.

You see, with mothers generally being the primary caregivers in the home (which is also the default role attributed to them by the patriarchy), your mother is meant to provide you with all the emotional and physical support for you not only to survive in this world but to thrive. If survival is the aim, it is aiming for the bare minimum.

Over and above the bare minimum that mothers are required to give their children, there are other needs that need to be fulfilled, the first of which is safety. Whether you have children or you are just paying attention in a public space, take a look at a child that seems to be in distress. Whether they have just dropped their ice cream cone or they are walking through somewhere that is darker than normal, their immediate inclination is to lift their arms and be held by their mother.

When you consider how big the world is for a small person, there are a lot of sources of fear for them. There are a lot of overwhelmingly large things that can be a source of anxiety. And with imaginations as creative as a child's, they may fabricate fears in their own minds. In such cases, mothers serve as a source of consistency, stability, and a safe space (Cloud & Townsend, 2013). Mom would never do anything to intentionally invoke fear or anxiety in their child. And yet, so often, it is mothers who are the source of the fear in their children.

Beyond physical safety, children—especially young children who have difficulties regulating and understanding their own emotions—need protection from the vicissitudes and the uncontrollable stresses that life inevitably brings. They need someone who will help them control, understand, and manage their emotions (Nania, 2017), and who better than the person who housed them within her own body? This protection and security in the formative years set the tone for the rest of an individual's life.

Secondly, children need to be nurtured. When I say it's a need, I don't mean it is something that children feel they are entitled to. The need for nurturing is so intense that babies or children who have been institutionalized have died from the lack of a mother's nurturing (Cloud & Townsend, 2013). The need is so intense that it too can be chalked up as a need for survival.

To nurture your child means to feed their soul with love, goodness, kindness, and discipline. It means loving them while guiding them and teaching them what is right and what is wrong.

Thirdly, your child needs someone they can trust. If a child has climbed up high and they ask their mother to catch them, they often won't think twice about jumping because they know, more than anything in this world, that their mom will catch them. That is a trust that has been learned. Mothers earn this trust by responding to their children's needs time after time.

The example of a child doing a trust fall with their mother is the most basic form of trust. But as they grow older, the trust they invoke goes deeper. It is trusting their mother with their fears, their secrets, and their problems, and knowing that even if their mother cannot solve their problems, she will at least lend a listening ear.

In the cases of children who fail to develop trust with their mothers, they may never climb to that height in the first place. They will nurture and protect themselves from the very person who should be protecting them.

Lastly, every mother needs to provide their children with a place to belong, and they need to be the person who can be an object and giver of love. Being wanted, being someone who is loved by their mother, and being someone who deeply and intensely loves their mother makes a person whole. It gives someone a place to not only belong but to actively take up space and fill that space with a whole and uncompromised version of themselves.

We see these basic needs well-established throughout life and history. This is what every child needs to thrive, to be well-adapted, and to be successful in every other relationship in their life. But for those of us who have been deprived of this basic affection, we are forced to live in survival mode.

But this allows us to look at the mother wound through a different lens. It allows us to look at the norm, the expected, the way mothers are supposed to relate to their children. And when we look at the concept of the mother wound through this lens, we can see just how distorted and unnatural this is.

Knowing that the mother wound is a generational burden (Goop, 2017) that is passed down from generation to generation, one has to beg the question of whether or not it is intentionally passed down, or if mothers constrain their daughters and clip their wings unintentionally because that is all they know and because it is what they were taught.

Does the mother wound exist beyond western society? You see, the idealization of the mother wound seems to be most prominent at a time when fulfilling this idealization was rife in western society. It was this society that so strongly harnessed and wielded the mother wound. What is the power of the mother wound outside of western society?

Modern lifestyle brand Goop (2017) covered the topic in-depth with family practitioner Dr. Oscar Serrallach, whereby he stated that the concept of the mother wound hasn't been created and established in modern society. Instead, it dates back to ancient Greek and Mesopotamian cultures, as can be seen in the stories of Penelope and Inanna. Further, he says that it can also be seen in archetypal stories like Cinderella. There is an unfortunate history of "unprotected, disempowered, and uninitiated women" (Goop, 2017) that goes far beyond the boundaries of modern western society.

The source of the mother wound can stem from two channels, either a passive or an active source. In terms of a passive source, young girls may witness their own mothers conforming to the constraints of society; they may witness their mother strictly adhering to the ever-so-high societal expectations, and in some cases, they may even witness their mothers buckling under the pressure of these expectations.

The active source of the mother wound is mothers actually teaching their daughters that relationships with others, and indirectly, the opinions of others, are paramount and are what determines a woman's success in life. If being your true self jeopardizes these relation-ships, then women are taught that they will lose the approval and even the love of their mothers (Nguyen, 2021). This conditional love, based on the relationships and opinions of others, can cause intense emotional difficulties when they inevitably crumble.

If being who you really are will lose you the love of your mother, you may reject yourself to keep that love —a love that was meant to be given without this major price tag attached. And thus, the toxic cycle of the mother wound continues; you are left constantly trying to create ways to secure your mother's love, changing who you are to fit into her box, without her loving you unconditionally for who you really are.

Repressing your true self or disconnecting from who you really are to earn the love of your mother ultimately leads to a landslide effect of insecurity and unhealthy relationships and attachments, to yourself and to others. This is why we see anxiety, depression, low self-esteem, substance abuse, and strained familial, platonic, and romantic relationships in those who have experienced the mother wound (Nguyen, 2021).

Who Experiences the Mother Wound?

Now, while it has been established that the mother wound is deeply rooted in a patriarchal society, does that immediately mean that it is an exclusively mother-and-daughter occurrence? Does it mean that sons are lucky enough to be exempt from this?

The reason this question is even asked is due to the false belief that men, or boys, are not as emotional as women and girls. Boys need to be nurtured as much as girls, and the idea that showing emotion as a boy is a sign of weakness leads to emotional unavailability from the mother, which leads to a son experiencing the mother wound.

Men experiencing the mother wound by having an unrealistic view of themselves and their emotions, thinking that they aren't allowed to express their feelings and their emotions, falsely hardening their hearts, and thinking that they have no one but themselves to take care of their emotions, is a sign of distress that can also lead to emotional and relationship problems later in life.

IDENTIFYING A TOXIC MOTHER-CHILD RELATIONSHIP

Because of this lack of love and nurturing, and the constant emotional constraints in your life from your mother, you may not immediately know or realize that you have been lacking. This seems like the norm for you and you never truly realize how broken you are until you see the relationships others have with their mothers.

But there are ways for you to identify if you have had a toxic relationship with your mother. The reason identifying this is so important is because your mother not only sets the tone for your life but also how you will interpret and interact with the world on an emotional level, and that is a high-stakes game to play.

These are some of the ways you can identify toxic maternal behavior that is not over-dramatized by blatant exhibitions in television (Streep, 2019):

- Shaming and blaming—No matter what you do, nothing seems to be right, and the worst part is that your flaws or mistakes are usually magnified in front of others, highlighted for you to be ashamed of. The flaws and mistakes that are so often pointed out become the lens through which you view yourself.
- Guilt-tripping—Pack your bags because you're about to go on an adventure. If you do identify

the toxicity of your mother's behavior toward yourself and if you do address it or garner up the strength to talk about it, you are at fault, with your mother facing life-threatening emotional turmoil—and it is all your fault.

- Comparison—They don't say that it is the thief of joy for no reason. Whether your mother tried to get you to eat your vegetables by telling you that the child next door always ate theirs, or told you to pursue a specific career because that's the career your cousin was pursuing, or blatantly asked you why you couldn't be more like your brother—it may just have been her own need to fit in and be the absolute best— comparisons lead to toxic and manipulative aspects that create wedges between you and other family members, make you self-conscious and overly self-aware, and unfortunately set the tone for low self-esteem and constantly feeling like you're never good enough. Even worse, you feel the need to constantly compete, even when you're the only one that seems to be running the race.

- Passive aggression—Whether this passive-aggressive behavior is shown by a mother toward the other parent in the home and, as a child, you witnessed this firsthand, or whether it was directly aimed at you, either way may affect the way you regulate emotionally and respond to specific emotions and emotional stimuli. However, passive-aggressive behavior is usually subtle and, to identify it, you need to be especially attuned to what is occurring. Not responding, taking a long time to answer or fulfill someone's requests, being stubborn, and being pretentious are all signs of passive-aggressive behavior. Instead of outwardly and openly expressing aggression, those who are passive-aggressive do so subtly or internalize their aggression and frustration. If you've ever been asked by your mother if "you are sure that's what you're going to wear," then you have been on the receiving end of passive aggression.

- Gaslighting—Remember when your mom told you she would take you to get ice cream if you aced your exam, you did ace it, but you never got ice cream because she said she never made that promise? Gaslighting is when someone tries to make you question your own grasp on reality. While it is a manipulation tactic, its primary purpose is to try to get you to question your reality, and in turn, your self-worth and self-reliability. It is so easy to do to a young child and, once the foundation and habit have been established, it's easy to keep on doing it.

- Marginalized or mocked—In the same way that ancient soldiers would kill one slave to set an example for the others and to gain further power over everyone, it might be a similar concept if you were always made to feel as though your opinion didn't matter, what you said was stupid, or the way you behaved was the perfect example for how others shouldn't behave. I have found many people who are the youngest in the family, and even the only girl in the family, who have been made to feel that their opinion not only doesn't matter but isn't even worth being heard. This creates an inferiority complex later in life.

- Scapegoating—Whether you are always the one person that has the blame placed on them or whether each day comes with a new scapegoat, placing the blame on someone else allows everyone in the family, including the mother, to feel a false sense of elevation. In other words, the idea that everyone else would be better off without the scapegoat around becomes a common theme.

- Stonewalling or the silent treatment—This is basically trying to put someone in a box that doesn't exist. If your mother ever ignored what you said, spoke over you to avoid listening to you, or chose to give attention to someone else when you were also voicing an opinion, then you may have experienced this. The silent treatment can be deafening and when this forms the basis of a relationship with a young child, this is bound to create emotional problems later in life.

- Extreme hot or cold—This is when your mother is either in an extremely good mood or an extremely bad mood, but you spend your life taking a gamble on which version of her you are going to get, constantly walking on eggshells in the hope that you may catch a glimpse of her good side. Spending time with your mother can be confusing because you never know which of the extremes you are going to face.

Maybe we don't understand the magnitude of these toxic traits. After all, how would a child stand up to or correct this kind of toxic behavior when they neither understand that there is a name for it nor that it is toxic in the first place? Unfortunately, identifying and remedying these problems only come later in life when the damage is done. It is only then that we realize our internal voices and the way we talk to ourselves are mirroring our mother's voice—the most prominent maternal figure in our lives. The voice of our mothers becomes the powerful yet tiny voice inside our minds.

EXHIBITIONS OF A WOUNDED CHILDHOOD

Now that you have grown into an adult and you are realizing some discrepancies in yourself and how you relate to others, you may find yourself digging deeper into who you are and why you are a certain way. You may see evidence of your childhood trauma creeping into your adult life, your adult relationships, and even the relationships you have with your own kids. How can you look back on the origin of this trauma?

Above, we have identified some toxic traits that your mother may have exhibited toward you, which also includes treating you as an extension of herself instead of as your own person. You served as her trophy rather than being an actual person. But what are the effects that this may have had on you as a person? Let us take a closer look (Neo, 2022):

- You may find yourself being acutely aware of other peoples' feelings. You grew up in survival mode having to tiptoe around your mother's moods and feelings, and now this is something you do with others all the time. But this can be exhausting.
- You may have a great IQ and you excel at all tasks, but your emotional intelligence is extremely low. You see, growing up with a narcissistic mother means putting your own feelings on hold, disregarding what you may be going through, or putting others' feelings above your own at the expense of realizing what you are actually experiencing. You are so busy taking care of others' feelings that you forget you have your own to take care of.
- It becomes easier to self-project when it comes to blame and feelings of guilt. After all, being so attuned to other people's feelings means that you begin questioning everything you ever did and ever said to them in an attempt to find

out if it's your fault that they feel the way they
feel.

- You have poor boundaries, always showing up
  or never showing up, all in an attempt to save
  others from yourself. The preservation of
  others overcomes self-preservation.
- You may easily be labeled as someone with
  "mommy issues" because you're constantly
  trying to mend your relationship with her or
  others who have a similar role in your life.
- You develop insecurities based on unhealthy
  attachments, whether you are overly attached
  or cold and distant. You always think you are
  being too much or too little and this, in turn,
  negatively affects the relationships you have
  because you are always overcompensating.

This is hard not only to understand by yourself, but to
explain to others because from the outside looking in, it
appears as though you have a normal, healthy, and
nurturing relationship with your mother. Heck, you
were not even able to recognize this narcissistic
behavior yourself. But when you do figure it out, you're
met with doubt from others.

But you may also find yourself feeling isolated or
frozen, you have difficulty making any form of decision, and you always feel like you've done or you're

doing something wrong. The emotional turmoil may also manifest as inexplicable physical symptoms, and most of all, you may look in the mirror and not recognize the person looking back at you.

Now, what you need to do is look back on your childhood and examine any incidents that may have hurt you, that may be a cause or root of trauma, and compare it to any of the examples of toxic behavior described above. This will allow you to form a link between the behavior you experienced, the trauma you face, and the way you are currently exhibiting this trauma. By working backward, starting with the behavior you exhibit, we can draw a line to the root cause of the difficulties you face that stem from the relationship you have with your mother.

The relationship you have with your mother as a child or infant is so great that neither the world nor you as a baby, sees yourself as an individual separate from your mother.

In the next chapter, we will look at the narcissistic mother from a clinical perspective.

2

THE NARCISSISTIC MOTHER

Knowing and identifying that you are someone who has experienced childhood trauma at the hands of someone you love, no matter what form that trauma takes, can be an uncomfortable and unsettling realization. But it is a necessary realization nonetheless.

Drifting from moment to moment, relationship to relationship, being acutely aware that nothing seems to work out, can be frustrating. Finding out the cause of this and learning why your relationships never seem to work out is the beginning of your healing process. Bear with me though, healing doesn't happen overnight.

In this chapter we are going to delve into a clinical look and a clinical perspective of narcissism. It is all well and good to now know the root of your trauma, but that may still leave some unanswered questions about why your mother would have victimized you. It may help you better understand her, and who she is, if you know the root cause of her behavior. It may even help if you gain perspective and discover whether this behavior, no matter how unwarranted, was done intentionally or unintentionally. Therefore, the first step toward your healing is to educate yourself on why your mother would have done that to you.

While there is a thin line between narcissistic behavior and narcissistic personality disorder, they both reap the same trauma in their children. But let us look at both concepts first before we delve into narcissism from a clinical perspective.

Narcissistic personality disorder (NPD) is a very real mental health disorder. At its very foundation, it is something that is cause for great concern from a medical and psychological perspective. Anyone who suffers from NPD is living behind a veil of false confidence and an inflated sense of self. However, when looked at closely, beneath the veil is just an insecure person who crumbles at any hint of criticism.

They need to feel important. They need to feel like they are better than others, and if they don't, they may face world-shattering anguish. While they may act as though they are superior to others, and a great act it may be, they are fragile and vulnerable underneath it all (Schwartz, n.d.).

Because of this fragility, it becomes hard for these individuals to maintain the ruse that they are better than everyone else, and permanently avoiding criticism from people is not a realistic solution to avoid confronting one's low self-esteem and fragile view of self. This means that they do not function well, they do not integrate well into communities, and they avoid the ones they love the most, usually because these are the ones who are most likely to be brutally honest. And down the rabbit hole they fall, becoming more and more isolated, putting up an even thicker veil to avoid anyone from suspecting that anything is wrong, but finding that being alone means that they are alone with their own lowly view of themselves.

These individuals need help because, somehow, they are caught between feeling entitled and worthless all at the same time. They have to face feeling both superior and miserable (Schwartz, n.d.).

Narcissism, or someone who is a narcissist and who blatantly exhibits narcissistic behavior, is someone who does not suffer from a mental illness. These people are dangerous because they actually think they are superior to others. It is not a veil that they use for their own protection, it's who they really are.

They are not above being obnoxious because they really think that others are beneath them and that they are superior. They blatantly have no regard, nor do they care about, the feelings or situations of others. It is hard for them to empathize with anyone, and they feel entitled, showing admiration for themselves, and taking admiration from others no matter how deserving they may actually be.

We all know of someone who turns another's problem into an opportunity for themselves to be the hero. They are the type of person who will offer a helping hand just to make sure they can later point out that, "If it weren't for me, you wouldn't have gotten that far." The reason they are so dangerous is because that is who they really are: ruthless and superior.

They feel no shame or remorse (Schwartz, n.d.); it is often easy for these types of people to get into positions of power, and easy to exercise that power too. Now, when you consider that the default role of a parent is one of power in a child's life, when combined with being a narcissist, it leads to a destructive and unbalanced relationship that wreaks havoc. The one who is left to face the damage and pick up the pieces of their life is the child, who has suffered a lack of empathy and a lack of emotional availability at the hands of the very person who was meant to nurture and love them unconditionally.

While it may seem that I am dwelling on the problem of the person who created your trauma, this is, in fact, the first step of your own healing journey. Knowing and identifying the root cause of your trauma means identifying the root cause within your own mother. This may look different for others, but for you reading this book, it means gaining an understanding of why your mother treated you the way she did. With this understanding in mind, the healing can be holistic, and you may find yourself feeling something for your mother that she may never be able to feel: empathy.

NARCISSISTIC PERSONALITY DISORDER

NARCISSISTIC MOTHERS | 45

We now know that when a person suffers from NPD, they have an actual mental disorder. This disorder ultimately affects their career, their jobs, their finances, and even their relationships with everyone in their lives. If the attention, focus, admiration, or all things great and beautiful are not given to a person who suffers from NPD, they may feel like they are crashing and burning.

In the case of parenting, this presents many problems. Firstly, any attention that would have been given to you as a child needs to somehow be taken away from you and directed toward your parent. Your birthday, for example, isn't celebrated as another year of getting older, but rather as the anniversary of the pain she endured to bring you into the world. When they don't get the admiration and expected love that they so fervently think they deserve, they begin cutting people off, because the relationships they have with others are unfulfilling.

From a clinical perspective, those who suffer from NPD exhibit common symptoms. From what has already been mentioned—most notably the inflated sense of self, the need for constant admiration, the entitlement, and the superiority—those who suffer from NPD will very often bring to light their achievements. Whether this involves rehashing the past or constantly trying to show off new accolades at inappropriate times (when others are receiving awards), they need the lime-light to be on them alone.

Like the villain in every Disney movie, those who suffer from NPD tend to dream about a day when they rule the world—or where they experience unparalleled success. Because of this success that they believe they are ever-deserving of, they can't associate with those beneath them, and they need to be in control of a conversation at the very least, especially if they are not going to be the subject of the conversation. They are envious and arrogant, and they are not above stepping on others as a means to get what they want (Mayo Clinic Staff, 2017).

However, these very symptoms are mirrored by the fragility that lies beneath the mask they so confidently wear. They will snap if they are not treated in a way that they feel they are entitled to be treated. They struggle with relationships and cannot merely be a spectator at a social gathering. Criticism is their down-fall and they easily become outraged, take offense, or exhibit other irrational behaviors when they are the recipient of criticism—constructive or otherwise. These exasperated emotions are a tell-tale sign of their insecurities and they have a way of projecting their low self-esteem onto others by trying to make them feel less

NARCISSISTIC MOTHERS | 47

than when they receive any form of negative feedback themselves.

Knowing that they constantly fall short of perfection and their own impossibly high standards of perfection, these individuals often battle depression and are purposefully isolated from everyone by themselves and by others (Mayo Clinic Staff, 2017).

So what sets off NPD in people? What flips the switch that creates these outward-facing individuals who project their negativity onto the world? While a finger cannot be placed on an exact cause, there are environmental, genetic, and neurobiological factors that contribute to this disorder.

Believe it or not, extreme parent-child relationships can lead to the onset of this disorder. The very thing that has led you here may be the root cause for your mother. Furthermore, there aren't any major risk factors at which one can look that have raised suspicions about a person developing NPD. While it is more commonly seen in males than in females (Mayo Clinic Staff, 2017), your mother presents as the most prominent example of someone who displayed NPD behaviors in your life.

The difficult thing about NPD is all the secondary mental and emotional health problems that it creates.

Low self-esteem, coupled with sadness and depression, is a breeding ground for addiction and other unhealthy coping mechanisms. Unfortunately, many people who do get help from a mental health practitioner may only do so when it is too late, and they may only do so as a way of treating one of these secondary symptoms that have been caused by NPD.

What NPD Is Not

Now that we know what NPD is, let us look at what it is not. In a world that tells you to love yourself, glorify yourself, love your imperfections, and embrace yourself as you are, it is easy to confuse or blur the lines between what NPD is and what it is not. It is *not* a form of self-love. Instead, it is being in love with a false and overly inflated version of oneself and also knowing just how unattainable this version really is (Smith & Robinson, 2022).

NPD is not loving yourself the way you want others to love you, it is not being the best version of yourself, it is not even striving to be this superior version of yourself. It is a distorted and unhealthy relationship that one has with themselves, and it goes far deeper than the physical love that the world constantly tells us we need to harbor toward ourselves.

Overt vs. Covert Narcissism

Narcissism doesn't exist in either black or white. Rather, it exists on a continuum ranging from severe to bearable. Within this continuum, there also exist different types of narcissism. Considering how complex the human mind is, and that our mental faculties are neither tangible nor easily expressed or understood by others outside of our mind, we cannot allow ourselves to imagine that mental disorders are any similar.

Narcissism in itself is quite complex and unique in that it does exist in the mind, considering that it is a mental disorder, but it is actively projected onto those who exist in the same space.

Considering the varying degrees to which narcissism can exist, there are generally two types that most mental health experts focus on. The first type is overt narcissism which, as the name suggests, comes with all the display and outward expressions of narcissism. It is also called grandiose narcissism and it can be identified by specific behaviors such as being overly arrogant, pretentious, aggressive, self-assured to a negative extent, and extremely dominant in relationships and interactions.

These are the individuals who are easily identified as narcissists. They are the individuals who arrive with pomp and flair to every occasion, making sure to shift the light onto themselves in any way possible. It is usually quite easy to identify these individuals as narcissists based purely on their behavior.

On the other end of the spectrum, there are covert narcissists. These individuals exhibit behaviors such as being anxious and easily succumbing to depression. They are usually the individuals that you are afraid to be honest with or to speak freely with for fear that you may say something wrong and that their internal narcissism will make them withdraw and become completely self-absorbed with their insecurities.

These are the individuals that are harder to identify as narcissists because their narcissism is masked as meek behavior. They are self-absorbed by the sadness that they seem to think only they ever feel. They are the people in your life who phone you when you are in the middle of a crisis but they are vulnerable and needy and only their problems matter. They are the people who never truly know that you are facing a crisis because they never really ask how you are. "Woe is me" are the words that flow from their mouth, and you never truly realize just how narcissistic their behavior is until you identify what covert narcissism actually is.

How do you identify if someone, whether it is your mother or not, suffers from NPD? Well, the clinical way of identifying this disorder is by looking at a set of criteria that an individual needs to meet to be diagnosed with NPD. An individual needs to exhibit at least five of the nine symptoms that have been mentioned above and they will be clinically diagnosed as having NPD (Raypole, 2021). Let us look at those symptoms again:

- They have an inflated sense of self, extreme self-importance, and an elaborate show of pomposity.
- They dream only of their success and the attainable power.
- They are entirely convinced that they are special, but not in the way that we are all

thought to be. No, they believe that they are far more special than anyone else.

- They have a constant need for praise and admiration (this may be hard to understand in someone who exhibits covert narcissism but can be seen by them constantly wanting you to tell them just how sad their situation actually is, or they want the constant sympathy that they have already been receiving).
- They feel like they have a right to anything they demand.
- They don't mind using others as a way to get what they want.
- They don't have a sense of empathy and they can't sympathize with the feelings of others.
- With their ill intentions, they are often distrusting of others. With this, they are also envious and jealous.
- They are arrogant and they feel that they are far above others.

Exhibiting five or more of these symptoms consistently over a prolonged period of time in multiple facets of their life warrants a diagnosis of NPD.

However, they are not the people who you could gently nudge to seek professional help. They are also not the people who would listen to you, and if you do suggest that they seek help, well, that may be the criticism that unravels them.

While it may not be a physical disorder, it can present with complications that may not affect their physical well-being but can affect their interpersonal, emotional, and mental well-being. Some of the complications that people can face when they suffer from NPD are that they can face challenges and difficulties in their relationships with others, they can have difficulties in the professional areas of their lives, they may face depression and anxiety, they may abuse or misuse drugs and other addictive substances, they may face detrimental intrusive thoughts, and this mental and emotional turmoil that they have faced can manifest physically.

NARCISSISM IN MOTHERHOOD

Now, the examples above describe anyone you may have encountered with NPD. This, however, is a unique encounter when it comes to your parents. Narcissism is not only difficult to identify in your parents, but it is also difficult to come to terms with. Despite their behavior and treatment, they are still the ones who raised you and they are undeniably loved by you.

So, let us look closely at how a narcissistic mother would behave, and how, as a child, it would be so complex to be in this relationship.

Particularly in the mother-child relationship, narcissistic mothers tend not to view their children as individuals but rather as extensions of themselves. So while it may appear that these mothers are self-sacrificing, that they do absolutely everything for their children, the reality is otherwise distorted in that their children don't actually have the freedom to be themselves, to make their own choices or decisions, or to be heard. Instead, they are meant to blend into the backdrop of a life that entirely revolves around the parent themself.

This becomes even more complex because it will always appear as though your mother is doing everything for you. And while this is true, it is purely to gain attention for herself. You see, by being overly involved in your childhood and school life, she will appear to be the parent who is always there, admired by many as the mother who will do everything for their child. But that is exactly what feeds narcissism.

She is at every soccer match, plans every school dance, is at every PTA event, and is even head of the committee (Robinson, n.d.). But this is not for you, nor is it for your benefit. This constant looming mother figure is not only present in your childhood, but is there, imposing, all throughout your life.

As you grow older, you see her influencing your academic and career decisions, prompting you and encouraging you to pursue a specific degree or job because that is what she always wanted to study herself, or because it is what she studied. Every decision you make is either subtly or blatantly influenced by your mother over-advising or telling you to do something.

This, unfortunately, doesn't get lesser with time; it doesn't ease up because she is never truly finished molding you. And then, you have kids. And when you have kids, she wants to parent alongside you, even though you have a partner who is fully capable of helping you raise your kids. But just in the same way you are seen by her as an extension of herself, your kids are seen as a further extension, and they are seen as more opportunities for her to gain recognition and praise that will ultimately feed into her narcissistic tendencies.

But all these behaviors, actions, and the increasing involvement in your life are challenging to identify or to even realize just how unhealthy they are because the true motivation behind her actions is buried beneath a mask of self-sacrifice and good intentions.

However, given that narcissism is not clear-cut, there are different types of narcissistic behaviors and tendencies that your mother may exhibit. And given the types of narcissistic parents that exist (which we will look at below), your mother may not fit into just one category. Instead, at different phases of your life, she may exhibit different types of narcissistic behaviors toward you. As you grow and develop, so do her narcissistic exhibitions. These are the types of narcissistic parents that exist (Ineffable Living, 2022):

- The severely narcissistic parent. This is a dangerous type and is the narcissistic parent that is most likely to cause emotional trauma in their children. You see, these are the parents who need all the attention on themselves. The attention that you may receive isn't even accredited to them by them seeing you as an extension of themselves; no, instead you are seen as competition with whom they must fight to regain all attention. If you do present as someone who may take the attention away from them, they will hurl insults and subtle criticism that will not only hurt you but will redirect the attention either back onto them or onto your flaws.

- The control freak. Everything you do must be for the pleasure and happiness of this narcissistic parent. If you try to deter from what they want for you, you are seen as going against their wishes and against their desires. This often leads to them playing the victim. They use the ruse of wanting what's best for you.
- The overly enmeshed parent. It really is an entrapment of the child. In these cases, your parent tries to have no boundaries between you two. They are emotionally needy and they expect you to be the one to fulfill their emotional needs. Why? Well, because they raised you and they made sacrifices to get you to where you are, so you owe them—at least, that is what your parent will tell you.
- The parent who needs parenting. These are the parents who are constantly vulnerable, weak, anxiety-riddled, overwhelmed, depressed, and addicted. These are the parents whose children had to step up and take on the role of provider and protector for the parent who needed it, but also for other family members.
- The parents who neglect. These are the parents who don't have a single speck of love or compassion within them. They are the ones

who, as long as they are taken care of, it doesn't matter what detriment their children may face.

The Harm of These Relationships

While the negative effects that these types of narcissistic relationships may have on a young developing child are quite obvious, and while it's quite clear to see the negative effects these relationships could cause right into adulthood, it would be remiss of me not to discuss the harm that these relationships can cause in a child.

No matter what age a child is, the negative effect of being raised by a narcissistic mother is quite detrimental. Not only are they hard to deal with in real-life interactions, but they also cause prolonged harm that reaches deep into the other elements of your life outside of these parental relations.

Considering that parental relationships form the bedrock of all other relationships, if this is built on a shaky foundation like with a narcissistic parent, it filters into every other relationship that a child may have. In romantic relationships, friendships, and professional relationships, the harm caused by parents seeps in and causes feelings of distrust, abandonment, fear, and loneliness. This causes unpleasant relationships and ones that never truly allow the individual to fully commit.

These relationships also create a platform that leads to behavioral issues. These individuals act out more often; inconsistencies from the parent create negative impacts on a child's behavioral patterns, and these negative impacts are not just present in childhood but throughout life (Loggins, 2021).

Lastly, being established in childhood, the one thing you carry with you into adulthood is stress. This is not the stress that keeps you motivated to complete tasks and to work hard. Instead, this is toxic stress that may even lead to learning impairments and negative impacts on mental, physical, and emotional well-being, and leads to these effects being present for the long haul.

While NPD does require a medical diagnosis, having this information on hand is important for you to figure out if this was what you experienced in your childhood. Without the knowledge of *what* a problem may have been, there is no insight into *how* to remedy the problem.

3

THE "F" WORD—FORGIVE

How many times have you heard that the only way for you to move on and be happy is if you forgive? How many times have you heard that if you don't forgive someone, they rent a space in your heart and your head, and the only one that suffers is you? And how often have you rolled your eyes every time someone has said this to you?

For the longest time, forgiveness was an abstract concept that I could neither understand nor wield. I kept wondering if I have the power to forgive someone, doesn't that mean I have power over them? I kept thinking that if my mother knew that I had forgiveness to give her, she would immediately grasp the idea of what she had done wrong. She would immediately drop to her knees, begging me to give her something that she never even asked for... But that is also when I realized that the hardest thing to forgive is an apology that was never heard.

So many times people have told me that forgiving someone was the key to moving on and healing. And much like you, I rolled my eyes in derision. The concept of forgiveness equating to letting something go was incomprehensible to me. But even deeper than that, a part of me didn't want to let go of the pain and hurt. You see, for the longest time, I defined myself as being a person who was broken by their own mother. Who was I outside of that hurt and pain? I was terrified to go through the entire process of learning about myself all over again, and that meant that I didn't want to forgive, I didn't want to heal. But forgiveness, as hard as it is to come by and to give out, was needed for myself and for my mother.

I needed to forgive myself for the guilt and doubtful feelings that seemed to constantly cast a shadow over everything I did. The constant second-guessing myself was the first thing I needed to gracefully usher out the door.

So, while I know that this is not something you want to do or something you may not even think you need to do, forgiveness plays such an important part in the healing journey, and after identifying the problem, it is the next step.

The first part of forgiveness is forgiving yourself. Some may say, "You didn't do anything wrong, why would you need to forgive yourself?" And while this is true, you will soon realize that the feelings of inadequacy that your mother so strongly instilled are usually what leads you to believe that you are responsible for the negative things that have happened in your life.

Forgiveness is far more complex than someone doing wrong by you and then you forgiving them. It starts with self-forgiveness, which is usually the hardest type of forgiveness that exists because let's be honest, how often are we willing to admit to ourselves that we have done something wrong? But when you realize that forgiveness is needed for all the negative self-talk and the negative inward voice we constantly use with ourselves, you realize just how much forgiveness we need to give ourselves.

This becomes even more complex when we realize the internal voice from which the negative self-talk stems sounds a lot like the voice of our mother. Therefore, to fully achieve the healing you are hoping for, you need to find a way of letting go of the feelings of guilt and shame.

POST-NARCISSISM FORGIVENESS—STARTING WITH YOURSELF

When you realize what has been taken away from you as a child who was raised at the hands of a narcissistic mother, you may find yourself wounded, cowering away from every form of intimacy for fear that each relationship may scratch at the open wound left behind by your mother. This may leave you feeling like so much has been taken away from you, and so much has been damaged and bruised within you, that you couldn't possibly be whole again. But that is why healing is a journey, not a destination.

The reason self-forgiveness is so important when healing from the effects of a narcissistic childhood and a narcissistic mother is because a direct comparison can be drawn between a romantic relationship and a parent-child relationship. In an abusive romantic relationship, you can entirely remove yourself from the toxic environment. But when this abuse comes from your mother, you may find it even harder to separate from this foundational relationship. That is why you need to seek comfort from within.

Let us draw a parallel between narcissistic romantic relationships and narcissistic maternal relationships.

The Narcissistic Partner

Having previously covered the behaviors and the relationship dynamic between you and your narcissistic mother, it would be quite easy to apply this to a romantic relationship. The reality is, you wouldn't immediately recognize them as narcissistic. Their confidence is attractive, the way they carry themselves is what draws you to them, and it's too late before you realize their controlling and emotionally abusive ways.

They devalue you, gaslight you, and everything in between, and you suffer immense emotional turmoil at their hands. They constantly manipulate you, and when you try to speak to those who care about you, you get the feeling that they don't really understand you. It's always responses like, "He never deserved you in the first place," or "He was such a loser from the beginning," or "I never liked him anyway," or even worse, "Just get over it."

None of these words ease your suffering and pain, and none of it makes you feel like those closest to you even remotely understand what you're going through. And once again, the person that you are is both grateful for that, considering that they have never experienced the turmoil you are currently going through, and you're a bit resentful about it too (yet another thing that you need to forgive yourself for).

As hard as it is, you can walk away from this person and from this relationship. But this is the person you chose. This is where the first form of self-blame comes in. You may feel that you allowed this to happen to you and that is why you can't forgive yourself. And when you do actually decide to leave, you hold yourself accountable for not leaving sooner. You blame yourself for not escaping. However, it is not that simple. As easy as people may make it seem, walking away from someone that you chose for yourself, and that you undoubtedly formed ties with, is extremely complex. The consequences of leaving a relationship aren't all good and self-love. Instead, it is tearing up a home and family if you have children, it is the logistics of assets, and it is the emotional loss of trying to mourn someone who hasn't died. It is a unique grief that you live with.

Through all of this, the concept of forgiveness lies almost entirely out of reach. After all, there are so many little things that you need to forgive yourself for now: for staying in the relationship, for not allowing yourself to escape sooner, for allowing them to treat you this way, for complaining about the hurt, for living in turmoil... The list is almost endless.

So where do you start?

When you step back and get out of your own head and heart, even for a split second, you realize what we now know about narcissists. Beneath the grandiose showcase of superiority lies someone who is extremely hurt. You identify the narcissistic traits in them and you piece together a puzzle that forms an image of a broken and weak person. You look at them and realize that all the hurt and pain that they cause you are just a reflection of what they feel toward themselves. And suddenly, you find yourself feeling sympathy for them. How can you hold a grudge against someone who is so broken, battered, and bruised? Before you know it, your heart leaves you with no option but to forgive them.

But even after you come to the realization, you still have a lot of self-directed blame that makes it even harder to forgive yourself. If we are being entirely truthful, it is always easier to forgive someone else than it is to forgive yourself. You may also find new things to blame yourself for even after you decide to forgive your partner. How could you allow their brokenness to affect you? How did their vulnerabilities somehow become your responsibility and your shame to deal with? Eventually, you get stuck in a place of realizing you still love them despite the heartbreak they caused you, and you are frustrated with yourself because of that too.

How do you get out of this vicious cycle? It's quite simple when you allow yourself to ponder it—everything you once directed at them, you are now directing at yourself. This is not a cause-and-effect type of feeling. Instead, it is a constant that what you feel for them, you feel for the parts of yourself that have bonded with them. You feel resentment toward them, and you feel it toward yourself too. When you realize that you still feel love for them, even though you forgive them and they have no place in your life, you can allow yourself to feel that same sort of love for yourself.

When you realize that there is no shame in love (Ann, 2022), it is easier to love yourself and forgive yourself too. You see, when you forgive yourself, it's not a matter of wondering who you are without that person. Instead, it is realizing that you have the opportunity to reinvent who you are. It is the same idea as knowing that when you hit rock bottom, you have nowhere but up to go.

So how do you even begin this self-forgiveness? When you think about it, not forgiving yourself actually serves as a form of self-preservation. You choose to not forgive yourself because it means facing all the trauma and the difficulties you have to go through that ultimately caused the damage. If you think that you were the one who got into this relationship and so you need to be held accountable, you are the person who did wrong, or there is a part of you who allowed this "wrong" to happen. Instead of forgiving that part of yourself, you lock that part in a box, inaccessible to the world. Only the good and perfect remains, the side of you who was untouched by the tainted love of your narcissistic partner. But this "good" side of you that exists, that is left untainted for the world to see, is incomplete and has no room for imperfection. That's a lot of pressure to place on yourself.

Yes, forgiving yourself is hard and it takes excruciatingly long to achieve, let alone understand. And when you are faced with the overwhelming emotion of the past trauma all you may want to do is close that part of you back up into the box. But if you stick with it, and you face those emotions, you realize that there is a wall in front of you, and on the other side of that wall something amazing is waiting. Forgiving yourself brings the wall crumbling down and on the other side is a new relationship that you get to have with yourself.

Getting to this point is weird because who defines the confines of self-forgiveness? Forgiving yourself is not just about letting yourself off the hook and hopping back into toxic relationships despite knowing the effects and the red flags. The tricky thing about forgiving yourself is that it may seem more superficial than real until you start feeling it deep within the confines of your heart. Verbally telling yourself that you forgive yourself isn't deep and meaningful, until you start believing it and you feel the breakthrough deep within. This is the most glorious feeling, but it is the hardest one to achieve.

Once you realize that forgiving yourself is not just the words you repeat to yourself over and over again but is rather the feeling you get in response to these words, breakthrough, no matter how uncomfortable it feels, is within reach.

But now, how does this translate to the narcissistic maternal relationship from which we can't escape? The relationship with your mother is the destructive relationship that leads to future destructive relationships. While romantic relationships have a start, the relationship with your mother doesn't have a start because it has existed since you were born. For that reason, it doesn't have an end either. How then can you forgive, when distance and escape aren't truly an option?

Forgiving Your Mother

What do we know about forgiveness? Whether it is rooted in advice or religion, it is always marked as a necessity that is required for an optimal life or optimal healing. Is it really the *need* that it is made out to be? We already know that forgiveness means nothing if it is superficial. Saying you forgive your mother for the sake of just saying the words means nothing. It has no meaning if it is not genuine (Robins, 2020).

So do you *need* to forgive your mother? No. It is neither a necessity nor is it probably your desire. But finding forgiveness for her will not let her off the hook, it will rather help you! Please don't be mistaken, I am not giving you an out or a way to hold on to your hurt and unforgiveness, harboring your pain even further because you read it in this book. It goes much deeper than that.

The reality is that the wound left behind by your narcissistic mother may never truly fade. And if that realization isn't enough to motivate you to hold onto the feelings of pain, then every hurtful word and action your mother has ever said or done to you is all the motivation you may need. But this is not where your healing intends to lead you. This is not your destination. Instead, when you understand that narcissism is a limitation on your mother's part, you find a feeling of empathy toward her. This empathy develops into forgiveness.

Ultimately, no one can tell you to forgive. And if the concept of forgiveness is pressed onto you when you are not ready to forgive, it won't be sincere. But when it does come, it will set you free in ways you have never imagined.

Whether you are ready for forgiveness now, or in ten years' time, it comes almost naturally because you get to a point where you want to thrive and live a full and happy life. You can't do that with an infection of hurt and pain that has been planted by your narcissistic mother. You find yourself naturally outgrowing the hurt and the pain. Forgiveness not only inevitably comes into your reach, but it becomes easier to open your grasp and let the hurt go. In the absence of hurt, forgiveness fills the spaces with its warmth, like liquid honey sweetening the bitterness that was left behind.

Forgiveness is not needed, but it is important.

As important as it is, it cannot be rushed.

Whether you have a child or not, I want you to notice a parent-child interaction where a parent needs to correct the behavior of a child. Perhaps they did something inappropriate and whether the parent yells or reprimands the child, notice that it doesn't take long for the child to go running back into their parents' arms as if they weren't just on the receiving end of discipline.

As children, our need for survival is dependent on our parents. This means that no matter what wrong they do, or what mental, emotional, or physical harm they cause us, we are inclined to almost automatically forgive them, no matter how much to our own detriment that hasty forgiveness may be (Hall, 2022). And so, in an attempt to forgive them *quickly*, we don't take the time to forgive them *properly*. This is where a parent-child relationship holds far more complexities than a romantic relationship.

You are intrinsically linked to your mother, since even before you were born. As much wrong as she does, you have a feeling of "she can't do any wrong in my eyes." And you will say this, with tears streaming down your cheeks, clenching the heart that she has just broken once again, in an attempt to cover the hurt that she has and will continue to cause you because we need our parents. It is how we are designed. This is the reason it's so hard to forgive your mother.

You may even find yourself making excuses for your mother. I know this seems strange to hear because you're probably thinking that you would never make excuses for her. But these excuses become so subtle that we don't even realize we are making them. You may find yourself using the following excuses (Hall, 2022):

- Children blame their parents for everything wrong in their life. This is not true. We don't want to blame our parents, and if you really think about it, our parents are the ones we tend to complain *to* rather than complain *about*.
- We chalk up their mistakes to "being human," and we all make mistakes; therefore our parents make mistakes too. We forget, however, that the narcissistic behavior and emotional abuse that we suffer for prolonged periods of time at the hands of our mother is not a mistake. The same mistakes don't happen every day for a lifetime.
- We try to justify our parent's behavior by blaming their childhood. We tell ourselves and whoever else will lend an ear that our mother

does what she does because she had a hard childhood. Does that mean you need to suffer for the circumstances of your mother's childhood? Does that mean two ruined childhoods are better than one? No.

- You tell yourself that your parents made sacrifices for you, they raised you, clothed you, and fed you. But we forget that this is the minimum requirement of parenthood and it does not warrant and erase the abuse side of the ledger.

- You try to be the better person. You tell yourself that you are better than that, that you won't pay them any mind, and you won't lower yourself to deal with these issues. But what you don't realize is that this is, in fact, avoidance, and it is the very thing that stands between you and your freedom.

- You try to tell yourself that you didn't suffer abuse at the hands of your mother because abuse is physical. You also tell yourself that you would have never known about narcissistic behavior if you hadn't encountered answers at this late stage in your life. But this begs the question of whether ignorance is bliss.

- You tell yourself that your mother doesn't know any better, she can't control her behavior, her actions, her words, or worse, you think that "this is just who she is." Don't ever mistake a narcissistic person for being ignorant. They know exactly what they are doing and they use their behavior as a weapon, wielding it against those closest to them.

- You try to convince yourself that your mother never meant to hurt your feelings. You tell yourself that her words weren't her true intention. But knowing that she had the option of not saying those words makes this a moot point because she intentionally chose to do and say certain things.

- Lastly, you try to make an excuse for your mother with the idea that your kids need grandparents. If your mother could emotionally abuse you, is that what you want your own children exposed to? You may argue that she is different with your kids. But is she different with you? Remember, your child feels for you the way you feel for your parents, no matter how warped and distorted your relationships may be. At the first sign of negativity they see exhibited by your mother, they will start harboring resentment toward her. Don't place your own kids in a position where they feel like they need to protect you.

It is understandable why you as a child would go to such extents to make excuses for your mother. You love her, no matter what she has done to you. But it's only when you stop making excuses do you realize that this is the only way to achieve healing. Holding people accountable and responsible for their actions allows you to stop blaming yourself.

When you actually step back and look at forgiveness, I mean you really look deeply and you try to conceptualize what genuine and true forgiveness is, some things come to light: You realize that it has nothing to do with the other person. Forgiving someone doesn't need to include telling someone you forgive them. It is an extremely internal and personal experience. Next, you realize that forgiveness isn't some automated trigger or switch that goes off in your mind where suddenly you are a person who has forgiven. Instead, it happens so slowly and so gradually over time until one day, after many days, weeks, months, or years, you realize that you're fine. You have these scars and bruises, but this is who you are. You accept that this is what has been done to you, and you are a greater person because of it. You are made up of the sum total of all the experiences you have had, the good and the bad. It is when you accept this—the scars, the hurt, and the pain—that you can let go of the excuses, accept the reality, and come out on the other side of forgiveness (Hall, 2022).

HOW TO FORGIVE

On this basis, you know that forgiveness is not for your mother's sake, but for your healing. It is simply a stop on the journey toward self-love. It helps you to not hold others in your life accountable for the damage caused by your mother. Your partner, children, and friends get a full and whole version of you, rather than the broken and bruised version left helplessly behind by your narcissistic mother. So the question is, with all the information that you now have, how do you forgive your mother? Let us go through some steps (The Relationship Notes Team, 2022).

1. Step One: Sort out the mess in your mind. Let's be honest, suffering trauma hardly ever means that your thoughts are all neatly compartmentalized and that you have a full understanding of every interaction you've had with your mother. Chances are, you had a moment of beautiful intimacy with her and you were left feeling confused by this interaction, guilty because you feel confused, and strange because this is not what you are used to. You may feel anger, guilt, frustration, and even sympathy, but with your mind's cup filled to the brim, spilling unwarranted emotions into every area of your life, you have no way of even considering a healing journey. First, organize your thoughts. What did your mother do to hurt you? Why do certain instances stand out more than others? What do you love about her? What do you hate about her? Get everything out on paper. Whether you are a writer or not, having your thoughts and emotions on a tangible piece of paper makes it easier to grasp and understand the mess in your heart and mind. If pictures and doodles are the way you best organize your thoughts, then make use of them.

2. Step Two: Create some space between you and your mother. While it may seem like this step is telling you to avoid your mother, this is not true. Avoidance doesn't heal, nor does it make the problem go away. Instead, putting some space between you and your mother is what you need to effectively sort and organize your thoughts. You see, with the space, you reduce any new forms of abuse that you may experience, allowing you to deal with what already exists rather than adding more to the problem. You may feel guilty for this space, but in the long run, it is necessary for you to pull yourself toward yourself while leaving behind the negative parts that your mother has tightly bound to you. You are not an irresponsible child, you just need this!

3. Step Three: It's so easy to blame yourself... Stop! You are not the cause of your mother's pain, but unfortunately, you are the effect of it. There is nothing that you could have done differently to change the way your mother treated you. The quicker you realize that it was not you, the quicker you can stop blaming yourself, and the quicker you can hold her responsible for her actions. Why? Because you can forgive someone who is responsible and

accountable for their actions, but you can't forgive someone when you're blaming yourself.

4. Step Four: Realize who your mother actually is. The fake love and doting mother role that she plays so well is nothing more than a mask that dwells on the surface of the endless narcissistic depths that lie beneath. Realizing that is who she is, that you can neither change her nor take the blame for her actions, makes it easier to pursue forgiveness.

5. Step Five: Learn to love yourself. Whether your mother falls on the extreme end of the abuse and tormented your entire existence, or whether she wasn't that bad, your worth and the love you have for yourself should not be defined by the terms that she has set in place. If this is so, then you will always be empty, lacking, and craving the love you need but don't think you deserve.

6. Step Six: Forgive your mother. But is it really that easy? Well, you have reached a point where you have come face-to-face with your feelings; you have acknowledged their existence, wrestled with them, fought with them, and when you consider that forgiving your mother means letting go of those feelings, you may be

in a better place to let go than you were when you started going through these steps.

7. Step Seven: Let go of the anger. While still a feeling that you are working through, anger is different. It wreaks havoc on your entire life. It is easily triggered, and you may find yourself angry all over again at your mother, allowing all the emotions you have just let go of to flood back into your heart. It is a gateway emotion and the better you deal with it, the better you can heal and forgive.

8. Step Eight: Find gratefulness. I know this may seem weird, but you wouldn't be the person you are today without your mother. This introspection that you are doing, the healing journey you are on, and the person that you are to your family and friends, wouldn't exist without all the experiences you went through, from your mother or otherwise. Be grateful for that.

9. Step Nine: Seek help. If you find yourself still unable to move from the point you currently find yourself in, if forgiveness seems impossible and your heart feels like it will never be ready to forgive and move past this, it may be time to consider speaking to someone who can help

you through your trauma on a professional level.

Don't allow yourself to wallow; forgive yourself and then move on because as comfortable as it is to stay with all the emotions, it really isn't meant to be your home. It's like sightseeing; you're just passing through, not taking up residency at the top of a mountain.

Remember, as hard as it may be, you can both love someone and need closure for the trauma you faced at their hands. Relationships are complex, but if they weren't, we wouldn't be as delicately and intricately woven as we are.

Now that you have gotten past the stage of forgiveness, let us work on loving yourself.

4

YOU ARE ENOUGH

Martyrdom and self-sacrifice, while greatly admired, are not all that they're cracked up to be. Being the child of a narcissistic mother, you may have found yourself constantly needing to sacrifice yourself, not for the greater good but just for the good of your mother. You have constantly been shifting, depleting yourself, to accommodate your mother. You may have depleted yourself so much that you are running on fumes, the remnants of what you used to be, just a shadow behind the ever-imposing figure of your mother.

Now is the time to change that narrative. Now is the time for you to realize the importance you hold in your own life. While you should have been playing the main character in your own life, you have been the under-study to the person who was meant to place you on a pedestal. But you need to understand how precious you are, how important you are, what position you deserve to take in your own life, how to increase your self-esteem, and how to get rid of the insecurities that have been so deeply embedded in your heart and mind.

You need to see that you are enough. Reading it here in this book is not enough to convince you. Hearing other people tell you that you are enough wouldn't be enough to convince you. But saying it to yourself over and over again, like a mantra, is enough to get you to believe it.

You are enough!

Say it again, louder for the deep emotional wound lurking in the back of your mind to hear it. Write it on your mirror so that you see it staring back at you every time you look at yourself, creating a neurological link. Remind yourself before you go to sleep, and when you wake up, tell yourself not just that you are enough but "how" enough you are. Add a quantity to it, a value. It is then that you will realize your power, and it is then that you will realize that you are all you will ever need.

Don't get me wrong, you do need other people. But you need yourself, and you need yourself to be full.

THE WAY YOU HAVE BEEN DERAILED

You know the feeling of hearing your mother subtly disarm and insult you in front of a group of people; it feels like you have been hit by a truck, you don't know how to respond, and you sit there not knowing what to say in response, so you take it all in instead. On the drive home, you are alone and you have time to wrestle with the occurrences that have just transpired, and you immediately get the perfect response. *Why didn't I just say that? That would have been the perfect response!* You think this to yourself but the moment has long passed and the damage has already been done.

Narcissists have a way of doing this to us. They have a way of hitting us with subtle blows that leave us with no retort and leaves them feeling like they have won. And perhaps in the moment, they may have won. But because they have won in their eyes, does it necessarily have to mean they have won in your eyes too?

You see, this is the greatest modus operandi of a narcissist and they use these tactics of subtle blows to derail you, catch you off guard, and throw you off your game. In doing so, they slowly take away, brick by brick, pieces of your self-esteem. You don't know if you can trust yourself anymore, you lose confidence in yourself, and what was once your certainty becomes your self-doubt.

But how do they manage to catch you off guard so often? How do they leave you without a response so often? How do they manage to derail you time and time again? Well, because you would never say or do the malicious things that they do, you don't know how to respond immediately. You are not plotting or scheming your next malicious response that will take anyone down. That is not the intent that you approach life with, and that is already what sets you apart from the narcissist.

Their charm, confidence, and outright boldness are enough to disarm you at the expense of losing your own self-esteem. While your love and kindness are often what cause you to fall at the hands of a narcissist, this should not be the reason you become cold toward the world. Instead, this is an opportunity to see just how valuable and needed you are. In a world that is crumbling in pain and darkness, you are the light. You don't have a malicious response to your mother, who told you that you looked fat at Christmas dinner, because you genuinely thought she looked beautiful in the new red dress she was wearing.

Now, you may be asking what this has to do with your self-worth and self-esteem. Well, you have been moving in this world with blinders on, your sight and views have been molded by the negative talk that came from your mother. Because she constantly derailed you and caught you off guard with nasty comments, you began believing it and this has led to low self-esteem. All the negativity that you continue to feed into yourself stems from the emotional abuse that you have received from a very young age. But how can you know better when all your mother fed into you was how wrong you were?

I have seen many people attempt to bury the deepest scars caused by the emotional abuse, or brush it off as nothing because "it happened a long time ago." They try to use the notion of time healing all wounds as a way of covering up the hurt and trauma, completely unaware that the emotional abuse experienced at the hands of a narcissist can have long-term effects. This is even more tragic when you consider that the abuse comes from someone from whom you cannot escape and who probably fed you this abuse on a daily basis every day of your formative years.

Emotional and psychological abuse at the hands of your mother can cause you to experience complex post-traumatic stress disorder (PTSD), which is where you experience some symptoms of PTSD coupled with emotional irregularity symptoms (Mind, 2021); you become codependent, and because you have constantly been receiving a deficit of validation, you actively seek it from other people in your life, making you extremely codependent. With your low self-esteem, you become an easy target for other narcissists and you are easily drawn into their false sense of validation. And the cycle of trauma continues further and further down.

While many people do try to create the illusion for themselves and others that they are long over the past trauma and that it has no hold over them any longer, the reality is that this type of trauma that follows you from childhood can have permanent effects, the scars of its grasp left visible for a lifetime to come. If left untreated and unaddressed, your trauma will cause you to lose yourself, leaving you in a place of never recognizing yourself.

With all of this that has been established, perhaps the question of *why* has stayed in your mind. Why would your mother, or anyone for that matter, intentionally or unintentionally treat another person this way? Narcissists beget narcissists. At their very core, narcissists themselves have very low self-esteem. The best way for them to make themselves feel better is to make someone else feel worse. In your mother's mind, the only way to take the attention off her imperfections and flaws, of which she is extremely insecure, is to point out and draw attention to someone else's flaws.

They do what they do to gain control of a situation, and what better way to control someone than to make them doubt and question everything they think they know about themselves in the form of gaslighting?

When you consider that a narcissist does not have the emotional capacity to feel for others, you can understand why they thrive by invalidating your feelings. They don't have the capacity to be vulnerable, and whether they see that vulnerability as a fear or a weakness, because they try so hard to hide it themselves, you may find that they use it as a defense mechanism against others. Narcissists are all about getting the upper hand on someone who they perceive to be a target. I know, when you're reading this outside of the concept of a shaky parental relationship, it can sound a bit malicious. But the reality is that this is a power play that narcissists use to gain control. When you are doubtful and insecure, they have the power.

Just in the same way, they also feel entitled—entitled to dictate your feelings, entitled to take control of a moment they were never meant to be involved in, and entitled to control those around them. They also feel entitled to every moment that happens in other people's lives. This can easily be seen in the way your mother needed to control every aspect of your life, every relationship; she had to be involved in every school project and event and she used this as an opportunity to take center stage in everything that happened in your life. Your life became the stage on which she was the leading act.

But why do they need to make you doubt yourself so much to gain power? The honest truth is that narcissists will try to gaslight you and make you doubt yourself, even if you aren't a perceived threat to them. For example, if you have siblings but it was always you on the receiving end of your mother's malice, you might find that at a family dinner or an occasion where you and your siblings had friends over, your mother would inflict her wrath on your siblings for no reason at all other than to assert her power.

The reason narcissists may feel fulfilled and empowered by making you doubt yourself is that they believe they are more important than you are. The mere definition of narcissism is that they think they are better than you, more important than you, and that while the world revolves around them, you are just another planet in their orbit.

With all of this that has been dumped onto you, the weight placed on your shoulders by the difficulties that stem from what should have been your most loving and supportive relationship, like a building torn down, you now need to go through the rubble that remains, and build yourself up brick by brick. And through all the hurt, pain, abuse, and trauma that you have experienced, you can know that you will have self-love and self-confidence that are nothing like that of a narcissist because you know better, and you don't want to be anything like your mother.

Bye-Bye Insecurities

We are all insecure about something; whether it is overly obvious or whether it is hidden beneath a veil of unseen emotions, there is always something that we don't like about ourselves. This dislike or insecurity usually stems from someone acknowledging this particular feature and shining a negative light on it. For example, the only reason you wouldn't really like your nose is that someone may have said something to you to point out how big or broad it actually is. You may not like your toes because someone pointed out that they prefer feet that look different from yours and now you don't ever wear open-toed shoes. Aside from someone pointing out your flaws, your insecurities can stem from your own mind, which has the power to draw comparisons between you and other people, and point out how greatly you fall short in comparison. As brilliant as our brains are, they can be liars at times. I know these examples seem superficial, but if these skin-deep attributes can alter the way we feel about ourselves, imagine how great the damage can be from what is left in the wake of emotional and mental insecurities.

Our insecurities can make us doubtful of everything we ever thought we knew. And this is because, as humans, we tend to linger on the negative more than we do the positive. At the very basis of confidence and insecurities lies the same foundation, the same duration, and the same level of effectiveness. Yet, the insecurities seem to give the confidence a run for its money. Whether you are carrying your insecurities from the past, or whether today you have faced something that has created a new source of insecurity for you, the reality is that this is something we all experience. Even the most confident person you know is insecure about something. Even a narcissist is insecure about something.

There are three types of insecurities that exist, namely personal insecurities, professional insecurities, and relationship insecurities (Waters, 2022).

1. Personal insecurities are the ones that exist at face value. They are the things we don't like about ourselves, that we assume others won't like about us, and are usually a physical attribute such as a facial feature or the way our voice sounds.

2. Professional insecurities happen in your career. They are present in this aspect of your life which is an extremely important facet. It is here where you will doubt your aptitude, where others can make you doubt your ability, and this usually leaves behind long-lasting scars that may even affect your performance in your career. It is here where you will come across

feelings of self-doubt and imposter syndrome, making you wonder if you were ever good enough for the job in the first place.

3. Relationship insecurity is when you experience feelings of not being good enough for your romantic partner. It is mostly present in relationships that you can choose to be in; for example, the chances are very low that you will feel insecure in a sibling relationship. But with a romantic partner, you may find yourself wondering if they could have made a better choice and have been with someone better, who deserves them, and who will make them feel as loved and as happy as they should be. If left unattended, these insecurities can usually be to the detriment of a relationship and often ends with extreme jealousy and controlling behaviors.

The Consequences

As the most important person in your own life, you set the tone for how people treat you, and most importantly, how you treat yourself. We often underestimate how important self-love and self-compassion are. But when we allow our insecurities to have control over us, we set the tone as being someone who doesn't need to be treated well; you open up the unsolicited opportunity for anxiety, depression, and mental health problems to seep in.

How do you overcome these insecurities? You need to change the narrative to begin setting yourself up for success rather than setting yourself up for failure. Acknowledge and confront your feelings, set realistic goals, and applaud yourself when you achieve these goals. Know that setbacks are inevitable, they will happen, but with the right mindset, you can overcome them instead of letting them overcome you.

The most important thing you can do is surround yourself with people and things that make you happy and that feed your soul. You will quickly realize that there are people who make you feel good, and there are people that take away from you, deplete you, and make you feel empty. These are not your people. The ones that make you feel most yourself, most comfortable, or that leave you feeling higher than you did before seeing them, these are the people who replenish you, these are the people that require no spent energy or effort, and who take you as you are. These are your people.

But even though we are surrounded by positive and negative people, it is important to know how to build yourself up, whether it is from the ground up, or just a little hiccup, and if an idea rhymes, you know it's a good one.

So how do you build yourself up? There are a few ways you can do that:

- The first thing you need to do is realize and affirm your value. It is easy for you to tell yourself that you are doing well, but you need to start believing it. Remind yourself of everything right that you do instead of everything that is wrong. Whether it is the fact that you drank water in the morning and you are now wonderfully hydrated, or whether it is the fact that you decided to help someone with a task, remind yourself of your value and your worth.
- Next, you are going to need to put yourself first. Now, there is a way of doing this without doing any less for others around. Often, we think that we need to prioritize others over ourselves or that we can't treat ourselves the same way we treat others. But this is not the way we should approach this. There is a famous saying that states that you can't pour from an empty cup. Do for yourself first before you do for others. It doesn't mean that you are self-

centered or self-absorbed. It rather means that you care enough about those around you to give them the best version of yourself. If you are feeling worn out, get a fresh haircut, take a break from social media, and talk kindly to yourself.

- Embrace the awkward and uncomfortable moments. Don't think too highly of yourself because you will fumble. But that's normal. Don't be too hard on yourself and accept the mistakes you may make.

- With that said, you will have negative thoughts. It is up to you how you deal with them. Challenge them, fight them; they need to fight to earn their spot in your mind, and if your positive self-talk overcomes those negative thoughts then they clearly don't deserve to have a space.

- Remove yourself from toxic situations. This means removing yourself from the negative interactions that happen with your mother. When you feel a toxic comment looming, remove yourself from the situation.

- Allow yourself to think back on the good moments, the positive feedback you've received from a client, the compliment your partner has given you, and the joy you felt when you spent time alone.

- Do the things that make you happy and bring you joy. Choose this over the things that take your joy away.
- Most importantly, don't try to do too many things at once. Yes, you want to get your nails done, do your hair, and go shopping for new clothes in the name of self-care, but with a looming deadline, it doesn't make sense to do this all in one day. Baby steps are important.
- Listen to your body and your stress response. Your body can pick up on vibrations a lot faster than your physical senses. Trust your gut.
- Toot your own horn. If you experienced a success, talk about it and don't downplay it. There is a difference between pride and being proud of yourself. Be proud of yourself.
- Change the narrative of your life. Only you can make this change. It is change that is required after you have lived a life of insecurities. You can decide that you will lead your life with confidence as opposed to living your life cowering in the shadows for fear of not being good enough.

DEVELOP AN ACTION PLAN

You can read about how to transform your life, but reading about it is nothing compared to putting it into action and taking actual steps toward changing your life. So here is what you are going to do: First, you are going to identify your insecurities. This is going to be so easy to do because you are already entirely and completely aware of these insecurities. Next, you are going to write them down, but for each one, you are going to make a *positive* note about why they are untrue. If you are insecure about your weight, remind yourself that you drink the amount of water that you are required to drink every day. Whatever you're insecure about, you're going to destroy it with a positive counterpoint. You are going to actively change the negative narrative with the positive one and, instead of dwelling on the negative insecurity, you are going to focus on the positive. Repeat it to yourself over and over again until you are so full of positivity that the negativity has no space to occupy your mind.

If your insecurity is that you can never be good enough, your positive statement can be that you are good enough because you are a human being. By virtue of you being a fully functioning person means that you are good enough. Your worth and value are not measured by what you do, but by who you are. Your existence is enough.

If you are insecure about your ability to successfully complete a project, your positive comment could be that you wouldn't have been selected for the project if you weren't good enough.

Now that you have discovered and tapped into the vein of confidence, and you spend every day overcoming your insecurities, it is now time to protect that confidence. Now is the time to set boundaries.

5

BUILDING YOUR BOUNDARY WALL

Daring to set boundaries is about having the courage to love ourselves even when we risk disappointing others.

— BRENÉ BROWN

To an outsider, setting boundaries may seem like you are brutally cutting someone out of your life. It may appear as though you are being harsh, and some people may even accuse you of being self-centered and self-absorbed. But the reality is, to nurture this newfound breakthrough you have made in your life through the steps mentioned above, you need to be able to protect it.

Where you are now in your healing process is actually extremely vulnerable. Everything that you have worked so hard to achieve can easily come crashing down if placed in the wrong hands. And so, this means that little by little, you need to build up your defense wall that serves to protect your heart. If protecting yourself comes at the cost of cutting loose the people in life who neither value you nor appreciate you, then I would say it is well worth the break.

But how do you set boundaries, not just with your mother but with your narcissistic mother? The relationship dynamic, coupled with the personality disorder, makes everything far more complex than it already would be. You know how difficult it can be to set boundaries with an imposing maternal figure. With the birth of my first child, my mother came in with all guns blazing, wanting to be the one to do everything for me and my baby. And while I loved her and appreciated her for that, I enjoyed being alone with my newborn, navigating the complexities of breastfeeding without her standing directly overhead telling me that his latch was wrong. I needed the imposing figure to cease and desist without coming across as ungrateful after she had stockpiled my freezer with meals for the next three months. When I gently asked her to give us some space, I was met with more hysterics than my newborn gave me in the depths of the witching hour. "I raised you to be who you are and I did a good job of that. How ungrateful of you!" That was the emotional overreaction I was met with.

Back then, I didn't know what I know now. I tried to set a firm boundary which she utterly and completely annihilated. Needless to say, I never got to bathe my newborn alone for the longest time after that because once again, I gave in and I let her win.

You see, what I only realized long after this had happened was that regular boundaries, or the boundaries we set with other people, don't work with narcissists. Setting boundaries with them the way we would with other people usually ends up with them using it as an opportunity to turn the tables back on us and criticize us for being a poor example as a child, in the case of a narcissistic mother. Trying to set boundaries with a narcissist bruises their ego, and ultimately creates a platform that they can once again use to point out how inadequate they think you are.

The only way to establish boundaries with a narcissist is to get creative.

The general way you may be assuming you'd approach boundaries with your mother may be a method that worked with other people. Perhaps you found it to be effective with them and you thought that it should be effective where you need it most—with your mother.

The reason we set boundaries is to maintain a certain level of health, whether physical, emotional, or mental health. Unfortunately, as we grow up, we learn that politeness and societal interactions are the bedrock on which cohesion exists. We learn that some things offend people, and we often traipse through life trying not to offend anyone, even to our own detriment. Consider how easy it is for a child to tell you that they don't want to greet someone. Think about how easy it is for them to tell you that they don't want to see or visit a specific aunt or uncle. The blissful ignorance that they live in, untainted by societal pressures, is often what we as adults hope for.

However, in an attempt to protect ourselves and our overall health and well-being, we also need to realize that people can't sense what our boundaries are. We can't assume that they know what makes us uncomfortable. This means that, more often than not, you need to be clear and precise with your boundaries, what they are, and why they exist for someone to truly understand them (in terms of someone who doesn't suffer from NPD).

If you're anything like me, you utterly despise confrontation, and if setting a boundary felt remotely like a conflict, I would immediately step back. But boundaries are important and it is up to us to set healthy boundaries with our friends and family, our intimate and romantic partners, our coworkers, and even strangers. These boundaries are important to maintain balance in your life, so whether it is about personal space, your energy (emotional, physical, or otherwise), time, sexuality or intimacy, morals and values, or material possessions, you need to determine when to say no.

But having this ammunition in your back pocket is worthless with a narcissist.

THE GRAY ROCK TECHNIQUE

Whether the name gives the impression of an impassable force, or if the name itself is creative, this is a technique I came across and I was utterly thrilled and pleasantly surprised by its effectiveness.

While the term "gray rock" may bring to mind a looming figure, it also brings to mind an image of a backdrop—not anything outstanding or worthy of attention. It is something that blends in rather than standing out. Now, when you consider that narcissistic people tend to feed off of your responses to their triggering interactions, you realize why the gray rock method is so effective. When you use the gray rock technique in the company of a narcissist, you limit your interactions with them, being as neutral and unengaging as possible. You limit eye contact, interactions, and engagement, and you basically blend into the background so that you don't become an easy target, or a target at all, for the toxic person in your life.

Realistically, avoiding or entirely removing a toxic person from your life is not always an option. And when these interactions are required, you need to find a way of coping and protecting the progress you have already made. This is not to say that the gray rock method doesn't have any flaws, the two greatest of which are that you need to make yourself invisible for the sake of a toxic person, and the second being that if you are no longer the target, there is a risk of someone else becoming the target. While the ultimate hope would be that, since the narcissist isn't getting a response, they will give up their toxic behavior completely, you need to consider this as a moment of putting yourself first and protecting yourself from this toxic person in your life. You are not throwing someone under the bus to keep yourself safe, but you are realizing that you can't protect someone else unless you are in a place where you can protect yourself.

This is not you cowering away, but it is you creating a situation where their ammunition against you is both ineffective and futile. In fact, they don't even get the opportunity to pull it out of their artillery. In instances where you know you can't avoid the toxic person, like a family gathering where you know your mother is going to be present, gray rocking can be particularly effective. It can allow you to show up and do what needs to be done, without engaging in any of the toxic interactions.

Basically, the way to use the gray rock method is to remain disengaged from the person who brings their toxic behavior to an interaction. You are going to be disengaged and distant no matter what because when you consider that the alternative is hoping no negative comments are hurled at you, when time and time again their behavior has proven otherwise, you can be sure that you are not risking behavior that would be thought of as rude. Instead, you are sufficiently preparing yourself against the onslaught that you are so used to receiving from this individual.

As with all good things and possible solutions to problems, gray rocking doesn't come without associated risks that need to be considered. There are negative psychological effects associated with this method which often involve you biting your tongue and suppressing any emotions that may well up inside of you to completely attempt to avoid the toxic person. Suppressing your emotions is never good and causes a buildup of these unexpressed feelings that negatively impact or affect your mental health. You may also find yourself feeling mentally drained and exhausted after an interaction with this toxic person because of the energy that is spent trying to control your responses.

However, what I have found, and my advice to you, is that you cannot reside here. The gray rock technique is a temporary tool to use, it is not a permanent solution that can be used when interacting with the toxic person in your life. Consider this, if you are an extrovert, disengaging and minimizing interactions with anyone goes against the fundamental nature of who you are. If you are someone who enjoys conversation and retorts, the gray rock method may cause you as much discomfort as the toxic behavior does.

My advice to you is to use this method when you are working on your healing, when you are focusing on building yourself up, finding your confidence, and establishing yourself outside of your toxic relationship. But once you have found yourself, you need to establish other healthy boundaries as a way forward. This comes with knowing when to use this method and when not to use this method. Using this method is great when you are working on your healing; it is not great when it leads to others becoming direct victims of the toxic person because you chose not to voice your concerns or confront the situation at hand.

Once you are in a space where you feel confident in yourself and your ability to safely separate from the toxic person in your life, you can establish boundaries by using your "no" effectively. And so when your mother points out that your hair looks untidy and asks you in front of everyone at a family dinner if you brushed your hair, you confidently respond with, "No, I didn't because I realized that my hair texture is a lot like yours and brushing it out would cause frizz instead of the beach look that I am currently successfully pulling off." Alright, maybe your interaction won't go exactly like that, but you won't have the fear of being caught off guard by any form of comment that comes from the toxic person in your life, and you certainly won't need to fade into the background to avoid confrontation.

So while the gray rock technique is great "for the time being," it is not effective in the long run and can prove to be detrimental to your own well-being if you depend on it too much. We want to establish boundaries, not a crutch for you to lean on. Let us delve into the ways you can set boundaries successfully, even with your mother.

SETTING BOUNDARIES SUCCESSFULLY

When you reach this point of setting boundaries, you are not just doing it to shield yourself from your narcissistic mother, but are also intrinsically creating a safe space for those you love and care about. Not only will you be setting a boundary that will prevent them from witnessing you suffer at the hands of your mother, but you will also prevent yourself from facing the suffering that ultimately takes away from you being the best version of yourself.

So how do you go about setting boundaries? Well, the first step would be to determine exactly what boundaries you are hoping to establish. Perhaps there is something in particular that your mother always seems to point out, maybe your hair or the career path you have chosen. Whatever it is, you need to be specific about what the line is and where it will be drawn. By being entirely honest and forthright, you remove any guesswork about what is acceptable to you and what is not. If there is more than one thing, you need to point each one out, because if each target they use is a bullet that cuts a hole into your emotions, you can imagine just how many pieces of you get torn apart with each new insult.

Next, you are going to lay the ground rules. Sometimes, being nice and polite isn't going to do the trick, and in the case of a narcissist, it is in their nature to test just how firm you actually are with your boundaries. Speaking to them once or asking them to stop and then leaving the issue at that is not always going to do the trick. Sometimes, you need to call them out privately or publicly if they are actively overstepping the line you have drawn.

NARCISSISTIC MOTHERS | 117

If you tell them that you don't appreciate them under-mining the career path you have chosen and talking about your earning potential in that field, you may find them slipping a snide comment into conversation. This is actually an opportunity for you to reaffirm what you have said. Point it out and tell them that this is exactly what you're talking about and this is what you want them to stop doing. They can't deny that they have done it because you are presenting them with an active example of what they do that you want to come to an end.

When you draw the line, remember that it is *you* setting *your* boundaries. This means that it is not open for negotiation or discussion, even though your mother may try. Setting the line means no compromise. It is also important to know that with a narcissist, as diffi-cult as this may be for you to do, there have to be consequences. Because if they try, and try they most certainly will, to push or break the boundaries you have set, there need to be repercussions for their actions. If it means they are no longer invited to any family function you host or they don't get to interact with certain aspects of your life, then that needs to be the punish-ment. It is also important that the repercussions that you set in place are upheld by you. They are going to test you and if you give in, nothing will change, your boundaries will be moot. Part of garnering your confidence is asserting yourself and making sure that your yes is yes and your no is no.

The chances of your mother appreciating these terms, or even liking them, are going to be close to zero. But after giving into her whims and preferences for your whole life, it is time to take the power into your own hands.

Ultimately, your narcissistic mother is going to see these boundaries as confrontation. She will begin using this as the new platform from which to hurl anger, hatred, and trauma at you. It is easy to get heated in the moment, but this is what every step in your healing journey until now has been preparing you for. Don't fight the narcissistic tendencies with hatred and anger. Remember forgiveness? There is a reason we worked on that before getting to this point.

Instead of responding with the anger and frustration that you are repeatedly pulling from the depths of your heart, you are going to remind yourself that narcissists feed off the reaction they get from you. That is why the gray rock technique is so effective as it involves no response at all. If they don't get the desired response from you, which is harsh retaliation, they can't play the victim as they usually do. For that reason, smile, shrug, or straight-out ignore their heated response that is used to get a rise out of you.

Remember that it is in their nature to do things to actively put you down, and while narcissists are all about the grandiosity of a put-down, they are not above taking subtle stabs at you in an attempt to push your boundaries or still achieve their malicious goals to hurt you. You have drawn a line and they are going to try to dance upon that line, gently swinging the pendulum either way to evoke something, anything, from you. By using smaller acts to poke at your boundaries, they may think that they can eventually break them down entirely. Calling out the behavior that feels like an attempt to test your boundaries is a great way to affirm and stand by your decision. Who decides if they are pushing your boundaries? You do. Any infringement of your comfort zone can and should be stopped immediately.

We are constantly told not to let the small stuff get us down, or to let the small stuff go, but this proves ineffectual with narcissists, who try to take away from you even more than they can carry.

If you consider that your entire relationship with your mother has felt like a battle, setting boundaries is going to continue to be a battle. It doesn't end here because they will constantly have the urge to slip back into their old behavior and you will regularly have to reinforce your boundaries. It is a constant give-and-take, but you can be the only one giving.

Now, something amazing may happen, and we can't allow ourselves to be so focused on arming ourselves against the bad that we forget about the good. Your mother may respect your boundaries and she may put in the effort to change. This cannot be ignored. Her attempts at trying cannot be left disrespected and unappreciated. With your boundaries still firmly in place, showing kindness and appreciation is a response to them respecting your boundaries. Go out of your way to invite them over, show them more appreciation than before, show them what all their years of narcissistic behavior has been standing in the way of, and give them access to your life in a way that wasn't possible before boundaries were established and adhered to.

With all that being said, there may come a time when boundaries aren't as effective as you have hoped, and you have to put distance between yourself and your narcissistic parent. If you need to do that, do it. Taking care of yourself is the only way you can take care of your relationships, so look after yourself and give yourself the self-care that you need. Sometimes self-care looks a lot like distancing yourself from toxic people.

The boundaries you set with your narcissistic mother may not be the same boundaries your sister would set with her. Boundaries look different for each person and the type of boundaries you set will be dependent on the result you are hoping for. When you do establish your boundaries, it is going to be something personal that you do for yourself. What those boundaries are and how you enforce them is entirely dependent on you!

Since we are creatively setting boundaries, let us also begin searching for creative ways to handle conversations and other interactions with your narcissistic mother.

6

TIME TO SPEAK UP

As humans, we are extremely dynamic; our ways of interacting with each other go far beyond telephone conversations or face-to-face interactions. Instead, we experience intrinsically complex interactions that are entirely different and unique to each person we know. You may even consider that everyone in this world knows a different version of you. This makes the fundamental basis of communication more complex than it would appear at face value.

Considering there are so many different streams of communication, it usually means that you have to deal with your narcissistic mother on more than one front. This can be overwhelming, to say the least, but finding a way of dealing with her during conversations and other interactions is extremely important.

Growing up with a narcissistic mother causes a unique trauma that is extremely complex for not only you as the sufferer to understand, but for anyone else to understand, even when you explain it to them. You are caught in an ever-swinging pendulum of needing to rescue yourself from her, while also constantly seeking her validation, love, and approval. But the reality is that you may never get these things from her. Knowing that this bare minimum isn't always easily accessible, we need to find a way of dealing with this void and finding a way of surviving our relationships without the possibility of ever getting these forms of affection from our mother.

Between forgiveness, setting boundaries that have the potential to be confrontational, and asking you to deal with the possibility that you may never achieve love and affection from your mother, it may seem like I am asking a lot from you. But believe me when I say that these are all paramount factors that need to be considered during your healing process. Here is the part where, after you have forgiven your mother and set boundaries with her, you learn that you are actually enough and that you are all you will ever need, even if she never showed that to you.

QUIET CONFIDENCE

How do you find enough, without being given enough in your formative years? How do you find enough in yourself, realizing that you hold everything you will ever need? How do you achieve this quiet confidence?

We know that confidence is essential for success and that it is usually a very attractive feature to have. But if you're anything like me, I have always found myself drawn to the masked hero, who comes in and makes a grand entrance doing something great, but without us ever truly knowing their true identity. The first appearance of *Marvel's* Black Panther before his true identity is revealed or *G.I. Joe's* character Snake Eyes always drew keen attention from me. I always wondered why until I learned about quiet confidence and that this is what they exude.

Quiet confidence is something that someone just has. They don't need to be boastful or in-your-face about it, but it is a surety that they have in themselves; they are confident in their abilities, and whether they say it or not, you know that they are beyond capable. They are the people who could command a room without saying much at all; they are the person whose reputation speaks for them; they are the person who does not need to boast because they know if they have to do something, their actions alone will attest to it.

Quiet confidence neither requires you to do anything to show your skill, nor does it require taking away from anyone else to prove your skill, aptitude, and superiority. In a strange way, having quiet confidence is the direct opposite of being narcissistic. While a narcissist wants to exhibit grandiose shows of their success and tell stories of how great they are, the quietly confident individual will clap the loudest for someone else, knowing that it doesn't take away from their abilities.

It is easy to identify quiet confidence when looking at a few traits in a person, and when you can identify it, you can also develop your own quiet confidence. But let us start with the former: How can you identify quiet confidence, and how does it look different from narcissism?

The way someone handles themselves shows you if they have enough confidence. It is usually the person who isn't trying to compete with others because they know that comparison leads to destruction. They have a certain sense of calmness around them and that is an aura that many find attractive.

Additionally, their body language also speaks for itself. Narcissists will try to be the loudest in the room, they will purposefully try to take up space—too much space —and they turn themselves into an exhibition rather than just being. On the opposite end of the spectrum is the person with low self-esteem. They try to shrink away from any attention and they try to occupy as little space as possible. The perfect middle ground is the quietly confident person. They hold their head up high, carry themselves with poise, make eye contact, and never seem to say anything unintentional or excessively rehearsed. They somehow always seem to find the perfect middle ground.

They command respect wherever they go, they're eloquent in their manner of speaking, and they have enough emotional intelligence to ensure they don't take offense when they aren't at the top of someone's priority list at a specific moment. With a strong sense of independence, they often find themselves perfectly fine being alone. They know that there is a difference between being alone and being lonely and they enjoy their own company enough to be peacefully alone.

Now, you may be reading this and someone in your life may immediately come to mind, or you may be sitting there wondering, "How do I achieve this level of quiet confidence?" You may find yourself wondering what people say about you behind your back. Well, there are ways to achieve this level of self-confidence. Remember that you can't take someone else's confidence and apply it directly to your life. Each person has their own unique way of commanding the attention that they uniquely deserve. An artist and a CEO, both the best in their respective fields, may equally exude quiet confidence but in entirely different ways.

So how can you develop your own unique brand of quiet confidence? There are two ways that you can achieve this. The first is unseen. It is you believing in what you are capable of and what your abilities are, having confidence in yourself, and understanding just how important your uniqueness is. This is usually unseen by the rest of the world and it is an unseen process. The second is the way you carry yourself. This is what the world sees and how the world responds to what you put out.

Let us delve into the first way, the inward-facing way of building up your quiet confidence.

1. The first thing you need to realize is who you are. You are uniquely purposed and positioned in this world. I know we hear a lot about uniqueness and how there is no one else like us in the world. And while this may get old real quick, it is extremely true. No one is gifted like you, talented like you, or capable in just the special way that you are.

2. Next, you are going to learn to love yourself at your worst. The quietly confident person is one who can be as comfortable with their successes as they are with their failures (of which there are many). You see, to be successful, you need to try and fail, and consistently try again, tweak your method and approach, and then you walk in your success. Loving yourself at your worst also gives you the assurance that when challenges undoubtedly turn up, you have what it takes to overcome those challenges with swift finesse because even if you don't overcome that challenge, you are still the same person who succeeded.

3. Having quiet confidence means knowing very well that there are good parts and not-good

parts about you, but also knowing that you wouldn't be a complete human being without these good and bad parts intricately and complexly wound together. Once you can accept the negative aspects of yourself, it doesn't mean that you need to stay that way; you can work on fixing them or even making them slightly better.

4. Something that comes with knowing the bad parts about yourself is understanding what your insecurities are. This doesn't mean that your insecurities are your bad parts, but instead, they are the things that you can be gentle with yourself about and work to improve. Gently run your palms over your life and pay a little more attention to the parts of you that cry out for love and that you sometimes deny.

5. Do what interests you, even if you are doing it by yourself. People may have expectations of you, like your mother may make a direct comparison between you and her best friend's son who's a doctor. This doesn't mean that you should pursue medicine to please your mother because you are going to be the one spending the rest of your life doing something you don't love. Instead, you are going to do what makes

you happy, what draws your interest, and what you enjoy.

6. Express your interests without fear. If you like painting, paint, even if you aren't very good at it; if you like to cook, cook for yourself and enjoy it, even if others think you aren't very good in the kitchen. Do something not for it to be good, but just because you absolutely enjoy it.

7. Surround yourself with like-minded people who are also quietly confident. There is nothing worse than mixing humble energy with someone who likes to be boastful.

8. Lastly, stick to your word and celebrate yourself when you achieve something. Let your yes be yes and your no be no, and when you achieve a goal that you were working toward, clap and celebrate yourself.

And remember that complimenting others and praising someone else's accomplishments and achievements doesn't take away from you.

Now that you know how to achieve quiet confidence within yourself, it is time to show your newly found confidence to the whole world. The first thing you can do is protect yourself from engaging in gossip and judging others. This is usually a group activity, and the group ends up pulling you down. Be the one to walk away from the situation and remove yourself from what is causing you the discomfort of engaging in negative talk about others. This is an actual physical act that will make you stand out from others. I am of the firm belief that if someone can speak negatively about someone else to you, they can do the same about you to someone else. Don't allow anyone to have the opportunity to say you engaged in negative talk about someone else.

The way you carry yourself—standing upright and tall, looking others in the eye when you're engaged in conversation, showing humor that isn't at the expense of others, and actively listening to understand others— is a way of inadvertently showing confidence, or quiet confidence, if you will.

If you are someone who always brings joy and positive energy to a room, you're going to be someone that people just generally love being around. If you outwardly express respect, are kind to people, treat others well, and smile often, it will directly affect how people interact with and perceive you. Lastly, don't be afraid to show your weaknesses and vulnerabilities; dress well, but dress for yourself and not for others, and develop your sense of awareness; you will find that people are immediately drawn and attracted to you.

Granted, the purpose is not to get people to fall in love with you, but to build up your own defense for when your narcissistic mother tries to attack certain aspects of your personality. But how do you use this as a strategy to deal with narcissistic parents or, more specifically, your narcissistic mother?

Firstly, the way you see yourself is the way the world, including your mother, will see you. She can't point out flaws and criticize aspects of yourself that you are already aware of, that you are working on, or that you have long accepted and embraced. With quiet confidence, people hold you in high regard no matter if you are at your highest or your lowest. In doing so, it eliminates the need for you to try, because you are constantly *you!*

This becomes a tool in your artillery because it is not an act that you put on, but it is who you actually become. You become and embody a confident person, and that is not something that is easily taken away from you, not even by the narcissistic comments that are frequently dropped by your mother.

Handling the Confrontation

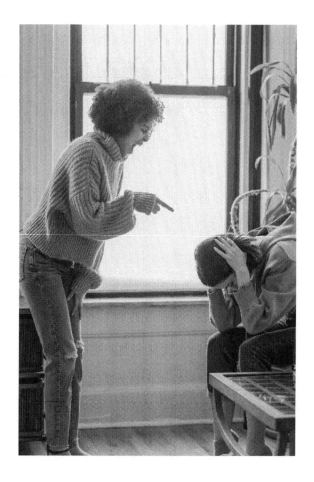

Something that you will notice about your mother's narcissistic behavior is that, while it does sometimes happen over text or the phone, it must regularly occur in live action when she is with you face-to-face. Whether this is because she doesn't expect you to retaliate when you're in a face-to-face confrontation or if it is because she has the most courage when there is an audience, it is usually during these interactions that you need to have the most confidence to combat her narcissistic attacks.

One of the key skills that you need to have to handle and deal with a narcissistic mother is to be able to handle confrontations. This was something I greatly struggled with because of how much I hate conflict. If anything seems to escalate or make an entire interaction worse and more uncomfortable, I am ready to remove myself entirely from the situation. But since this is when your narcissistic mother may hold the upper hand in a conversation, the best skill you can have is being able to disarm them of their weapon, which in such cases would be a negative or nasty comment.

We know there are moments where avoidance may not work with your mother and therefore, knowing what to say and when to say it may help you to minimize the negativity and verbal abuse that often subtly make their way into a conversation. Their whole purpose is to manipulate and gain control and this means they are often not ready for specific responses. They expect you to cower away in shame and humiliation, and when you respond, you throw them entirely off track.

There are different "disarm phrases" that you can use in different cases. If you find the environment to be particularly hostile and your mother's anger seems to be raging, the best disarming phrase may be to pointedly tell them that you are not engaging in a hostile interaction. Remember when we said that, sometimes, you need to be blatantly honest with a narcissist? In the midst of heated anger on their part, you may need to engage by telling them that you aren't going to engage. These are some phrases that you can use:

- Your anger is not mine to deal with.
- I don't like the way you are talking to me, so I will not engage in this conversation with you.
- I can't control what you are feeling right now, but you can.
- I am extremely uncomfortable because of your behavior. I am going to remove myself from this situation.
- I am not willing to engage in further argument.

In many cases, such responses will trigger immediate introspection which will usually lead to them saying that they didn't intend to come across as aggressive. But whatever their response may be, you will either be removed from the situation or your disarm phrase will have done its job successfully.

When your mother is engaging in subtle hostilities, trying to undermine you in front of others, and choosing an aspect of you as a point of shame and insult, this is when you could use different disarming phrases such as:

- Could we try to engage in respectful conversation rather than hurtful conversation?
- You are entitled to your own opinion.
- I can accept that you feel that way, but I don't feel the same way.
- Your perspective is interesting and I see where you're coming from. However, I must choose to disagree.

These are the types of responses that will immediately disarm them because, instead of gaining an upper hand, all you do is gently assert your quiet confidence. You point out that the flaw they notice or point out isn't a comment on who you are but on who they are.

Narcissists try to assert control and dominance, and more often than not, your mother will try to assert dominance over your life. She may subtly suggest the best path for your life, and whether she is imposing her hopes and dreams on you, comparing you to others, or trying to mold you into someone who lives up to the unrealistic expectation in her mind, the reality is that you are your own person. You are not an extension of your mother. In cases where she shifts the conversation purposefully in this direction, you can respond with:

- I can make my own decisions.
- We can agree to disagree.
- Please allow me to share my feelings.

While having a ready phrase is great, it is important to know when to use it, and in the right and appropriate context to use it, otherwise, you may find yourself in another moment where, on the drive home, you find yourself thinking, "Ah man, I should've used this particular disarming phrase."

When engaging with your narcissistic mother, you need to remember that while you are attempting to disarm her, the aim is not to engage. One thing that's certain is that narcissists love a fight, and in the heat of the moment, if you are not cautious, it may be easy to slip to their level and retaliate, causing the situation to escalate instead of disarming the situation. Also, they live for their ego. The point of disarming the situation is to neither feed into their ego nor bruise it, considering that it is already fragile beneath the hurt they are trying to inflict on you. In the midst of heated emotions, it is all too easy to give in to their emotions and try to take responsibility for them. If your mother is heartbroken and bruised by your boundaries—boundaries that have been set in place to protect you—you cannot be held responsible or liable for that. Knowing that this is the behavior that your mother may have used in the past, it is up to you to set yourself firm against playing the role of a martyr and taking on the responsibility of your mother playing the victim.

The Feedback Sandwich

Now that you have some disarming phrases on hand, the reality is that these aren't always effective. In the heat of the moment, it is all too easy to fall into the black hole of emotional quicksand and respond to your mother in the exact same way that she has been speaking to you. But two wrongs don't make a right. While you aren't expected to entirely disregard your own feelings, you need to be extremely mindful of the responses you allow to be solicited from you. This is because narcissists, being focused only on themselves, aren't even mindful or aware of what you are feeling but rather only about how they are feeling.

Knowing your mother, you may look at the disarming statements above and think to yourself that they are far too harsh, even for your mother. And this may be true if they are inclined to take offense at everything. But when used in the right way, in the form of a feedback sandwich, these phrases hold unmatched power while still being wrapped in the sensitivity that your narcissistic mother so deeply craves.

If you consider that the disarming statements are actually a form of constructive criticism for your mother, then a feedback sandwich offers this constructive criticism neatly and politely wedged between two forms of positive feedback. This is more likely to prevent a conversation from escalating while still providing your mother with the exact message you need her to hear.

However, just like any other sandwich, if any part of it is laid on too thick, the balance is entirely thrown off and a peanut butter and jelly sandwich becomes an almost entirely jelly sandwich. That is to say that the feedback sandwich method is also flawed and you do need to be aware of these flaws. The reality is that the feedback in itself may come across as too harsh if it is improperly presented. Your mother may nitpick and may choose to focus on that part despite your efforts of intrinsically including well-thought-out and elegantly executed positive comments.

While the criticism may be too harsh to be sugar-coated, the pendulum may also swing too far in the other direction, whereby the sugar-coating is too sweet for her to even notice the criticism that you need her to receive. Clarity is key, and the feedback sandwich may distort this clarity to a catastrophic extent where neither you nor your mother comes out unscathed on the other end.

While using this technique may make it easier for you to give the necessary response to your mom, it is important to strike the perfect balance of neither feeding her ego too much nor bruising it to a point of making the situation at hand far worse.

You see, the feedback sandwich—often used in work and professional settings—provides you with just enough distance to safely hold up the boundaries you have established with your mother. However, she is your mother after all and you hold an intimate bond with her that can't be solely based on you constantly trying to correct her hurtful behavior. This means that the positive comments that you use in your feedback sandwich go much deeper than they would in a workplace or professional environment where you are commending someone's outstanding customer interaction. Your bond and emotions run far deeper with your mother and so determining the correct criticism and positive aspects to present to her may be harder.

But here is where you can delve deep into your heart and tap into those complex emotions where you simultaneously love her and can't stand what she does. No one experiences your emotions the way you do, and sharing them verbally may be even harder. But when you realize that this is your mother, it becomes far more complex than just words and guided boundaries.

Every example and every possibility or outcome that I may present you with in this book, and every possible interaction that you may prepare for in your mind, may be futile at the moment when reality appears to be so vastly different. It is important to think about how you can use these strategies in the next interaction you have with your mother when the situation may inevitably turn out negative. Think about how you will implement these strategies, but remember not to hold any expectations because you can only control your responses, not your mother's. It may not be received well by her, and that's alright.

The next chapter will allow us to unpack and delve into the trauma bond that exists between you and your mother and how you can work toward breaking those bonds.

7

BREAKING FREE

Every bond we form with every single person we encounter, whether it is the person we fall in love with or the stranger we pass by on the road, meets a version of ourselves that is entirely unique to them, not just because of how we treat or respond to them, but also because of the way they perceive us. Each relationship and interaction we have is complex because of the way our minds create relationships.

One of the most uniquely fascinating relationships is that of a mother and child—a bond formed even before birth, mother and child are interconnected, and the fibers of their beings are woven together in a constant state of deep and intimate affection. It is a relationship and a bond that can neither be synthesized nor replicated. And when abuse exists in this relationship, it fundamentally pulls apart everything we thought to know and conceptualize, and we are left with tatters of what was meant to shape our entire life. This is a trauma bond.

All the advice you receive proves futile in the relationship you have with the one person you love and hate the most, the person you loved first and will probably love last, the person who taught you both how to love and how not to love.

But some of this advice is difficult to apply and even understand, given the complex emotional and psychological ties you have with your mother. People may tell you to just get over it, move on, and that you deserve better. But how would you know? She really is the only mother you have ever and will ever have. This advice can be easily applied to a partner that you move on from, but for someone to whom you are bonded forever? It's not like you can get over this mother-daughter relationship and move on to the next one.

And when you have faced a lifetime of narcissistic trauma, it is hard to stop fixating on your experiences; it is hard to move on, a part of you may not even want to move on, and when this is all you know, where do you go from there? Learning life all over again at the age you are can seem daunting and overwhelming, and we can't fully understand and comprehend the psychological bonds that exist. Maybe we were never meant to.

Therein lies the link that exists between a victim of trauma and abuse, and between the person who constantly and consistently inflicts that abuse.

You may have heard of it before—a kidnapper holds a person hostage for years, and eventually, the victim, although constantly exposed to trauma and abuse, becomes infatuated with their captor. They may actually fall in love with them. This is known as a trauma bond. The thing about trauma bonds is that you can feel so guilt-ridden by missing the person that emotionally traumatized you that you live with these feelings by yourself, facing even greater trauma.

Let us delve a little deeper into what a trauma bond is before looking at it in the context of the mother-child relationship. At its very core, a trauma bond is an extremely dysfunctional relationship where the victim gains an unhealthy attraction to the person who is the very source of their emotional trauma. This attraction need not be romantic or physical, but it can be a deep emotional attraction and even codependency of the victim, on the person causing their emotional harm (Adamo, 2019).

This emotional attachment forms the foundation and the basis of the relationship between a narcissistic mother and child. This type of trauma bond is particularly complex because not only does the victim, the child, not want to sever the bonds and ties that exist in this highly toxic and abusive relationship, but the very nature of the relationship also makes it extremely difficult to do. This relationship is unlike that which exists between a captor and a captive. In those cases, the captive is usually trained to respond to fear, they often knew what actual love was before being taken captive, and they know that what they are experiencing is abuse. But the negative so constantly and consistently floods their minds and hearts that it flushes out all the good that may have been previously established.

However, in the case of a parent and child relationship, this trauma and abuse form everything that the child knows about love and affection. They believe that this is what is normal and expected when they are actually facing an onslaught of abuse on a daily basis.

A narcissistic parent, being who they are, cannot change their behavior, and instead, when their child is born, they negatively groom their child into feeding their narcissistic tendencies. It is therefore seen that children will pursue higher grades or play the piano because that is what their narcissistic mother likes and prefers rather than what they like. When this is all a child knows and serves as the foundational source of what they expect love to be, they face endless difficulties later in life when the realization of what was actually traumatic dawns on them.

As you grow older, you may find yourself terrified and constantly wanting to avoid your mother, but you expose yourself to the negativity and trauma for the slightest sliver of positivity that may come from an interaction with your mother. You will risk exposure to every part of negativity in the mere hope that something kind comes from her mouth. And in most cases, because they know exactly what they are doing, they will throw that one piece of positivity deep within the abuse because they know that is what keeps you hooked, and is what keeps you coming back. Trying to break apart the harmful bond that exists between you and your mother is extremely complex. By mere virtue of you being their child, this trauma bond is rendered near impossible to sever because the lines that make you their child and their prize or property are deeply distorted. You defining yourself as your own person or cutting ties with your mother may be the most significant loss she suffers. You are not only taking away what she considers her property, but you are also taking away the power supply that feeds into her narcissism. Your mother will not relinquish control without a fight. And this is why the only way for you to cut yourself free from the clutches that so tightly hold onto your mind and emotions is to go through self-healing (Degges-White, 2021).

So how do you begin healing yourself and how do you separate the trauma bonds that aren't one-sided from your mother only, but are also deeply rooted within you? Well, the first thing you need to do is acknowledge that your feelings exist. Yes, it may only come long after the trauma has been at its worst. It may be you as an adult realizing that other people around you had very different relationships with their parents and that yours was the unhealthy one. This in itself is something that is extremely difficult. It is finding out that your relationship with your mother was not healthy. It is then acknowledging the feelings of hurt, betrayal, and pain. Just because you are the only one feeling these emotions does not make them any less real. Feel them, name them, acknowledge them.

When you do begin to face and confront these emotions, a twisted lie may form in the manner of your mother pinning the blame for this treatment on you. But you cannot be held responsible for their actions and the way they treated you. Your mother may try to pin the blame on you, but in the parent-child relationship, she was the adult who was supposed to set the tone for your relationship (Degges-White, 2021).

In your mother's futile attempt to pin the blame on you, comparisons may be further drawn between what you see with others around you and yourself. Again, this presents an opportunity for your mother to place and emphasize the blame on you that you were not good enough, deserving, or worthy of the love your friends may have received from their parents. This is yet another lie to deter you in your pursuit to sever the negative bonds that exist between you and your mother.

As you venture down the path of self-healing, it is important that you don't go too far in the opposite direction of a narcissist. Trying to please people more than you please yourself, not having any boundaries, and being codependent on others is a recipe for disaster and may nurture more negative narcissistic relationships in the future (Degges-White, 2021).

Lastly, expectation only leads to disappointment. If you have any expectations that your mother will change, the only person that will be disappointed is you. Instead, part of self-healing comes with the acceptance that your mother may never change, not even on your account.

From here, your journey is about separating from your mother without harming and hurting yourself. You need to start developing and building up yourself and your relationship with yourself. Distance, coupled with boundaries, is the best way for you to learn who you are without the abuse and, more importantly, who you are without the negative influence of your mother.

But how would you know if you are trauma-bonded to your mother? You may find yourself fixated on the past hurt and trauma caused by your mother or even other people. You may find yourself longing for and missing the very person that hurt you; you keep going back to the people who hurt you, almost drawn to them despite the pain they cause you. While your loyalty to those who hurt you is admirable, it is usually at your own expense and to your own detriment.

EXPECTED ABUSE

As someone who had a toxic relationship with a narcissistic mother, you may find yourself, despite being accomplished, well-to-do, and easy on the eyes, at the end of a string of failed relationships and you can't understand why.

I figured out, through lots of help, and watching a friend who also experienced trauma at the hands of an abusive narcissistic mother, that trauma bonds often prime their victims, which leads to failed future relationships.

Because you are trained to disregard your own boundaries, are tolerant of certain behaviors, and hold back on expressing your emotions, many people who have been victims of narcissistic relationships with their parents seem to attract narcissists as partners. Because they so quickly and easily fall into these defensive roles in a narcissistic relationship, the relationship tends to crumble to the ground. It is sort of like experiencing expected abuse, and this, in turn, prompts a partner to convey more abusive characteristics.

How do you break these trauma bonds that have ultimately primed you for ruined future relationships? The first thing you have to do, once you have established boundaries and established a safe distance between you and your mother, is to constantly remind yourself that you are safe. You are no longer in harm's way. You need to remind yourself of this until you begin believing it. If you are still in any trauma bond with either your mother or another relationship that poses any similarities in terms of the trauma you previously faced, then you are not, in fact, safe.

If you have come to a space where you have successfully moved past the trauma and you find yourself triggered by a similar feeling or even emotion, remind yourself how far you are removed from the actual trauma in both time and space (Adamo, 2019).

After playing it safe for so long, in an attempt not to risk yourself being hurt by your mother or any other relationships that may bear a striking resemblance to the traumatic relationship you had with your mother, you may find yourself entirely shut off emotionally, even toward yourself. The only way you can feel emotional fulfillment with others is if you feel emotional fulfillment within yourself. This will allow you to feel whole in yourself rather than needing to feel whole through someone else. Start with opening up emotionally to yourself. You know that you can never hurt yourself, so be emotionally available to yourself (Adamo, 2019).

Because of the trauma you have faced, you may find yourself extremely attuned toward the moods and emotions of your mother and even the narcissistic partners to whom you always seem to be drawn. Let's change this. Instead, turn the focus to yourself, and read your own cues as a way of getting to know yourself. You can only treat other people well when you know how you are going to respond, and when you are gentle and nurturing with your own feelings and emotions.

Lastly, you may find a way to rub your healing in the face of the person who hurt you. After all, how delightful might it be to tell your mother that you are doing well without her? What if I told you that this only negatively affects your healing? In fact, if you find you want to prove to the person who hurt you that you are doing fine, you may not have healed at all, and once again, you are trying to do something with them in mind rather than with yourself in mind.

While it won't be easy to do this, your future self will love and appreciate you. But along this journey, you may even find yourself facing withdrawal symptoms from the trauma that you have become so familiar with. As your body tries to adjust to a new normal, or a way of life that doesn't include the abuse that you are so used to, it will be uncomfortable. It is, after all, taking you away from everything you know. Fixating on the trauma and negativity that have passed, you may find yourself facing anxiety, being hyper-alert, and expecting the stimulus of the trauma to be lurking behind every corner (Adamo, 2019).

If you do come face-to-face with that trauma or you are forced to see your mother, you may find yourself feeling extreme forms of helplessness in the situation. You may also find yourself experiencing flashbacks because present stimuli rehash past trauma. You find yourself stuck in a cycle of overly feeling to a negative extent. This makes it harder for you to move on and, if you are not careful and taking care of your mental well-being, it can lead to depression, feeling like you are stuck in a deep hole that you can't get out of—a hole that has been dug by you and your mother.

When you go through trauma, your body deals with processes that happen in the moment and after. In the moment, you will experience either fight or flight, or you may even be entirely frozen. It is natural for us to replay these moments to learn how to better defend ourselves in the future, but this often results in living in a loop of replayed trauma which, as you may guess, is not good for your mental health.

Because of a fear that has developed as a result of this trauma, you may also be hypervigilant, either not engaging with many people for fear of getting hurt again, or engaging in relationships but never fully giving and committing all of yourself to a person. This both hinders your relationships and protects your emotions.

The only way to get out of these withdrawal symptoms is to consistently provide yourself with reminders that you are no longer in danger.

Using Affirmations

On your healing journey, you may not realize the benefits and beauty of using positive affirmations. Yes, these are just words that you are saying to yourself, but eventually, when you say them often enough, they become true.

Tell yourself that you are capable, worthy of respect and dignity, and that you are willing to open yourself up to trusting again. Tell yourself who you actually are and hold on to the truth of that tightly, not allowing anyone to tear your identity from your grasp. Remind yourself that you are safe and that you are enough. And most importantly, tell yourself that you will find peace and that you will protect that peace at all costs; after all, you worked far too hard to get to where you are now for it to all be squandered (Davis, 2020).

Now, it is time to move on to such an important part of the healing journey: actually healing.

8

TIME FOR HEALING

I have come to learn, through both hard and easy lessons, that although extremely personal, healing can only be achieved if you are properly supported. The hurt that lies deep within needs to first be uncovered, unearthed, and exposed to the light and love of the day. And only when you hold it in your hands, looking at it intently, can you gently open your hands and let it go entirely. Where the wound was will still be sensitive to the touch. You may even bandage it up in the hope that no one handles it too often or too much. But eventually, it scabs and heals. And one day you wake up and you feel okay. The mourning that you once felt, while still tender and present, isn't the gnawing pain you thought you had to live with forever. And just like that, you have achieved healing.

Healing for me wasn't a switch that flipped. No, instead, healing for me happened so slowly and so gradually that I didn't even realize I had achieved it at first. It wasn't until one day when I woke up living in the state that for so many months I had deeply yearned for that I realized I was healed. It was a phenomenal feeling, and when I realized that it had cost me time with my mother, I realized how deep the value of that payment really ran.

How do you achieve this healing that you are so deeply yearning for? While there isn't an exact order of steps that you would need to take to achieve healing, there are things that you can focus on to make it easier to achieve your healing. The first thing that you need to do, however, is be patient with yourself. You can't attach a timestamp to your healing journey because all that will do is leave you feeling disappointed that you haven't achieved your desired state by a specific time. Healing is not quantifiable, and as much as you might want to control things, the reality is that it happens at its own pace. Being patient gives you the opportunity to achieve your healing without a deadline looming over you.

With patience comes self-compassion. However, this can be hard to achieve, not only because we tend to be overly critical of ourselves, but also because we never established a genuine feeling of self-directed compassion from our parents. It may cause hurt to resurface, and it may cause us to be transported back to a time of trauma, but when you learn to be compassionate with yourself, you can truly nurture your healing.

You know the little voice inside your head that sounds a lot like your mother that is always pointing out what you have done wrong? You're going to work on that voice next. There is a part of you that may be constantly trying to live up to a version of yourself that your mother loves. But you constantly fail because every time you try, the little voice in your head points out why that will never be good enough for your mother. This little voice needs to be given attention and you need to argue with that voice. When that part of yourself tells you why you are not good enough, counteract it with the stronger voice in your mind pointing out why you are good enough for *yourself*. You will always have a comeback and a counterattack because that voice is you.

Having this little voice inside your mind and your heart can make it hard for you to trust yourself. After being primed and groomed toward being far too hard on yourself, it may be difficult to trust yourself. Like any relationship, you are learning yourself from scratch, you are starting fresh, and this means learning to trust yourself too. There is a scared and traumatized version of yourself deep within that needs to be shown that they can come out into the world and face what often seems to push them down. Allow yourself to trust yourself and you will be surprised at how happy and fulfilled you can be in your own body.

Take some time to practice self-care. For too long, you haven't nurtured yourself and you haven't felt the nurturing touch of a mother either. Now is the time to change that. The reality is that self-care for you may not look like face masks, spa days, and full-body massages. While these are forms of self-care, it is exactly that—*self*-care. Find what works for you. Seek what makes you feel replenished. If it is spending time alone reading a book, do that. If it is going on a walk with a group of friends, do that. Whatever allows you to fill your soul, do that. You deserve it after a lifetime of depleting yourself for your mother's sake. It is time to get full of yourself.

Healing from narcissistic abuse is not the same as healing from other types of trauma. There are things that you should be aware of as I mentioned previously, such as not having exact steps to follow. Healing looks different for everyone. While others may come out of their shell after they have healed, others may find peace and become even calmer. Everything is usually measured out in steps as a way for us to keep track of our progress in life. But the reality is that steps cannot be applied to everything. These are not steps toward recovery or steps for grieving. While these are all factors in the healing process, healing itself happens at very different paces.

Remember that the mere fact that you are on a "healing journey" means that you are delicate and fragile. I don't mean this as an insult, but rather, I mean that you are learning to navigate a life of healing instead of a life of hurt. This can be overwhelming in itself. This also means that you need to be hyper-aware of false comforts that actually cause more harm than good. What I like to do is actually limit social media during my time of healing or when I am trying to be kinder to myself. Social media has a way of either fueling the emotions within us or feeding us with false emotions.

Healing comes with certain complexities too. On this journey, you find out who you really are; your healing may lead to self-discovery, and you may fall in love with a version of yourself you never knew existed. However, on the journey of healing, self-love, and self-discovery, you may find yourself losing people who you thought loved you and you may find yourself forming unexpected bonds with new people. Some of the people closest to you won't understand your hurt and pain, and the reality is sometimes we're the villains in other people's stories. Perhaps to them, your trauma is your negative energy. It's fine. Some people aren't meant to be in our lives forever. But this journey is important. Just the way trees need pruning to grow, you may need to prune yourself from certain people in order to grow.

One other uncertainty that you also need to face on your healing journey is that you may never fully gain closure. But if you persist and continue working on yourself, it is fine if closure is never found. People say that you need to heal and forgive, lest you die with a broken heart. But what if *trying* to heal and *trying* to forgive is enough? You may never overcome the hurt. Does that mean you need to live life in a state of "given up" or should you persist to be the best version of yourself even when you don't feel like it? Healing, while it may never be achieved, should be constantly strived for.

SEEKING SUPPORT

There may also come a time on your healing journey when you realize that, though you are enough, you need the helping hand of others to get to a place of peace. Sometimes help can be in the form of a support group, a therapist, or even just a friend or loved one that may be the best shoulder to lean on.

I know, seeking professional help can seem extremely daunting. How do you know if you can trust this person? How do you know if you can share your hurt, abuse, and trauma without receiving judgment in return?

The truth is that you can't. Any decision that you make to seek help from someone means presenting your wounds and your vulnerabilities to a person you may not know in the hope that they treat it with the sensitivity you so deeply desire. Seeking help from a professional can be tricky because you need to make sure that narcissism trauma is their forte. Much like an interview process, you need to "shop around" for someone who you think will best be able to help you through your trauma. This may mean going through one person or five people before you find the one, and when you do, you may need to build your trust toward them.

You can ask your therapist certain questions to make sure they will add the value you are hoping for, such as asking them what their experience and approach is to emotional abuse, how this may differ or be adapted for narcissistic abuse, if they have worked on cases that are similar to yours, and if they provide care over and above the therapy sessions you have with them, such as scheduled or unscheduled phone calls (Atkinson, 2017).

You may also ask them what your expectations should be for the individual sessions and what your overall expectations should be; you may ask them what their experience is in dealing with cases similar to yours, if they serve as a guide or just an external consultant, and if they will give you advice beyond the scope of your narcissistic trauma (Atkinson, 2017).

Most importantly, you are going to need to trust yourself and your gut in the decision of choosing a therapist. Do you feel safe and does it feel "right" to pour out the intimate details of your life to this person? It is a decision that should not be taken lightly and one that you should pay close attention to. Take notes, scrutinize the decision, and listen to your heart. Unfortunately, some therapists are not trained to deal with NPD and they are unable to treat or understand their patients. So finding the right fit for your particular case may take a bit more work.

The good thing about the reality you are currently facing is that you are on the cusp of being made whole again. Is this journey going to be easy? No. Is it going to take time? It most certainly will. Will it be worth it? It will be worth everything your mind and soul are worth, and there isn't a price tag big enough in the world that is as valuable as your sanity. Healing is around the corner… Chase it!

CONCLUSION

With eyes full of tears and emotion pouring out of every part of my mind and body, I relinquished the control that both my mother and I had over my mind and heart. And with that came an intense breath of freedom. I was finally cut loose from the tethers that bound me so deeply to the hurt and trauma caused by the woman I loved so much.

This feeling of elation and pure joy is the same feeling I realized so many others like me deeply yearn for. After the emotional trauma and abuse came healing. It wasn't easy, but I am now strong enough to share with the world what worked for me, in the hope that it will work for you too.

Now, I face successes in my life on a daily basis, I have relationships with my children that are fulfilling and healthy for both them and me, I am emotionally available to my partner, and most importantly, I am happy.

As for my mother, she is very much still a part of my life, but with boundaries strictly set in place and deeply enforced (sometimes reinforced over and over again), we managed to find a healthy middle ground. Although it took a while, forgiveness came too. I may have fought the forgiveness, but it did come. In an attempt to protect myself, I kept reminding myself of the hurtful things she seemed to continuously do. But falling into that deep, dark place was a heavy burden on the relationships that really mattered to me. To be the best and fullest version of myself, forgiveness was inevitable.

From forgiveness to realizing my self-worth, from building boundaries and taking the lead in confrontation, and from breaking free to healing, I have gone through the steps and I have come out on the other end. It was long, hard, and terrifying. But those whom I love and who love me in return deserve a full and uncompromised version of me. They deserve to be loved by me in a way that I never truly got to experience. With that, I have also had to let go of the hope and unattainable dream of having my mother love me the way I yearned to be loved. Instead, I loved myself that way, and I set the tone for how others should love me too.

So while this will be scary, allow me to go on this healing journey with you. After all, we all deserve a happily ever after. This is where your story begins!

GLOSSARY

- **CPTSD:** Complex post-traumatic stress disorder is often seen when you experience some symptoms of PTSD coupled with emotional irregularity symptoms and disabling symptoms such as hypervigilance, anxiety, and intrusive thoughts.
- **Gaslighting:** A form of psychological manipulation that makes a victim question and doubt their own reality and perception.
- **Gray Rock:** A defense mechanism to approach toxic and abusive behavior by being non-reactive and dull in the presence of an abuser so as not to draw any attention to any part of yourself that can be targeted for abuse.
- **Mother Wound:** Generational trauma enforced by the patriarchy that forces mothers to teach their daughters to behave in a certain way to please others instead of themselves. It can lead to confusion and greatly affect the psyche of a young, developing girl.

- **Narcissistic Personality Disorder (NPD):** A diagnosable mental disorder that is usually characterized by an inflated sense of self and a lack of care and empathy for others.
- **Trauma:** Severe psychological or emotional hurt that has the ability to alter one's sense of self.

REFERENCES

Adamo, N. (2019, June 23). *Trauma bonding: How to release a trauma bond.* Natasha Adamo. https://natashaadamo.com/trauma-bonding/

Ann, L. (2022, January 16). *Finding forgiveness after narcissistic abuse.* Medium. https://medium.com/@lenabarnum/finding-forgiveness-after-narcissistic-abuse-9adae4b74487

Atkinson, A. (2017, April 29). *How to find a therapist who understands narcissistic abuse recovery & NPD: 10 powerful questions.* QueenBeeing. https://queenbeeing.com/find-therapist-understands-narcissistic-abuse-recovery-npd-10-powerful-questions/

Atkinson, A. (2021, June 26). *Why do narcissists make you feel like you're not enough?* QueenBeeing. https://queenbeeing.com/what-are-the-reasons-narcissists-make-you-feel-like-youre-not-enough/

Calvello, M. (2021, May 10). *The feedback sandwich: Should you use it? (Pros and cons).* Fellow. https://fellow.app/blog/feedback/the-feedback-sandwich-should-you-use-it-pros-and-cons/

Casabianca, S. S. (2021, February 15). *What is a narcissistic personality and can it be treated?* Psych Central. https://psychcentral.com/disorders/narcissistic-personality-disorder#overt-vs-covert-npd

Catchings, C. V. (2022, February 3). *How to heal from narcissistic abuse.* Talkspace. https://www.talkspace.com/mental-health/conditions/articles/narcissistic-abuse-recover-heal/

Cherry, K. (2019). *How to understand and identify passive-aggressive behavior.* Verywell Mind. https://www.verywellmind.com/what-is-passive-aggressive-behavior-2795481

Childs Heyl, J. (2022, June 23). *How to find a narcissistic abuse support group.* Verywell Mind. https://www.verywellmind.com/how-to-find-a-narcissistic-abuse-support-group-5271477#toc-seeking-support

Cloud, H., & Townsend, J. (2013, October 16). *Five things every child needs from their mom.* The Christian Broadcasting Network (CBN). https://www1.cbn.com/family/five-things-every-child-needs-from-their-mom

Crespo, R. (2021, November 7). *12 ways to exude quiet confidence.* Minimalism Made Simple. https://www.minimalismmadesimple.com/home/quiet-confidence/#:~:text=Quiet%20confidence%20is%20a%20quiet

Davis, S. (2020, June 29). *The trauma bond and healing from narcissistic abuse.* CPTSD Foundation. https://cptsdfoundation.org/2020/06/29/the-trauma-bond-and-healing-from-narcissistic-abuse/

Degges-White, S. (2021, May 12). *Breaking the trauma bond forged by narcissistic parents.* Psychology Today. https://www.psychologyto day.com/au/blog/lifetime-connections/202105/breaking-the-trauma-bond-forged-narcissistic-parents

Eatough, E. (2022). *Grey rocking: What it is and how to do it (and when not to).* BetterUp. https://www.betterup.com/blog/grey-rocking

Eddins, R. (2022). *10 simple ways to set boundaries with narcissistic parents.* WikiHow. https://www.wikihow.com/Set-Boundaries-with-Narcis sistic-Parents

Estrada, J. (2018, November 3). *10 pro tips for overcoming insecurity and cultivating unshakable confidence.* Well+Good. https://www.welland good.com/how-to-stop-being-insecure/

Evans, M. T. (2021, March 11). *Why you need to forgive the narcissist.* Narcissism Recovery and Relationships Blog. https://blog.melani etoniaevans.com/why-you-need-to-forgive-the-narcissist/

Goop. (2017, March 16). *Healing the mother wound.* Goop. https://goop.com/wellness/relationships/healing-the-mother-wound/

Hailey, L. (2022, April 15). *How to set boundaries: 5 ways to draw the line politely.* Science of People. https://www.scienceofpeople.com/how-to-set-boundaries/

Hall, J. L. (2022). *Are you rushing to forgive your narcissistic parents?* Psychology Today. https://www.psychologytoday.com/au/blog/the-narcissist-in-your-life/202204/are-you-rushing-forgive-your-narcissistic-parents

Hilton Anderson, C. (2021, May 18). *16 quotes about boundaries that will help you say "no."* The Healthy. https://www.thehealthy.com/mental-health/boundaries-quotes/

Ineffable Living. (2022, September 9). *Healing from a narcissistic parent— 7 practical strategies.* Ineffable Living. https://ineffableliving.com/heal-from-a-narcissistic-parent/#11-5-types-of-narcissistic-parents-

Kholgi, B. (2022, May 8). *15 best ways to boost quiet confidence (2022).* Coaching-Online.org. https://www.coaching-online.org/quiet-confidence/

Kovanen, M. (2019, March 26). *How does the mother wound impact men?* Dr. Mari Kovanen. https://www.drmarikovanen.co.uk/how-does-the-mother-wound-impact-men/

Lamothe, C. (2019, November 22). *How to stop being insecure and build self-esteem.* Healthline. https://www.healthline.com/health/how-to-stop-being-insecure

Lewis, R. (2020, September 29). *The mother wound: What it is and how to heal.* Healthline. https://www.healthline.com/health/mother-wound#signs-and-effects

Loggins, B. (2021). *What is a toxic mother?* Verywell Mind. https://www.verywellmind.com/what-is-a-toxic-mother-5204882

MacKenzie, J. (n.d.). *Forgiving yourself after narcissistic abuse.* Psychopath Free. Retrieved November 15, 2022, from https://www.psychopathfree.com/articles/forgiving-yourself-after-narcissistic-abuse.366/

Mayo Clinic Staff. (2017, November 18). *Narcissistic personality disorder.* Mayo Clinic. https://www.mayoclinic.org/diseases-conditions/narcissistic-personality-disorder/symptoms-causes/syc-20366662

McBride, K. (2016). *How a narcissist can derail you.* Psychology Today. https://www.psychologytoday.com/us/blog/the-legacy-distorted-love/201610/how-narcissist-can-derail-you

Miles, M. (2022). *Should you use the feedback sandwich? 7 pros and cons.* BetterUp. https://www.betterup.com/blog/feedback-sandwich

Mind. (2021, January). *Complex post-traumatic stress disorder (complex PTSD)*. https://www.mind.org.uk/information-support/types-of-mental-health-problems/post-traumatic-stress-disorder-ptsd-and-complex-ptsd/complex-ptsd/

Nania, R. (2017, May 19). *Why prioritizing motherhood in first 3 years is critical*. WTOP News. https://wtop.com/parenting/2017/05/why-prioritizing-motherhood-in-the-first-three-years-is-critical/

Neo, P. (2022, March 4). *12 signs of a narcissistic mother & what to do for true peace & freedom*. MindBodyGreen. https://www.mindbody green.com/articles/narcissistic-mother

Nguyen, J. (2021, November 28). *Understanding the mother wound, the intergenerational pain women inherit*. MindBodyGreen. https://www.mindbodygreen.com/articles/mother-wound

Parker, T. (2021). *How to disarm a narcissist (and make them a bit more tolerable)*. Divorce Magazine. https://www.divorcemag.com/articles/how-to-disarm-a-narcissist-and-make-them-a-bit-more-tolerable

Pomerance, M. (n.d.). *7 crucial things no one tells you about recovering from narcissistic abuse*. The Candidly. https://www.thecandidly.com/2019/7-crucial-things-no-one-tells-you-about-recovering-from-narcissistic-abuse

PsychAlive. (2015, January 23). *How to overcome insecurity: Why am I so insecure?* PsychAlive. https://www.psychalive.org/how-to-overcome-insecurity/

Raypole, C. (2020, July 27). *12 signs you might have narcissistic victim syndrome*. Healthline. https://www.healthline.com/health/narcissistic-victim-syndrome

Raypole, C. (2021, April 6). *9 formal symptoms of narcissistic personality disorder*. Psych Central. https://psychcentral.com/disorders/narcissistic-personality-disorder/symptoms#narcissism-diagnosis

The Relationship Notes Team. (2022, January 20). *9 steps to forgiving a narcissistic mother: A guide*. The Relationship Notes. https://therelationshipnotes.com/forgiving-a-narcissistic-mother/

Robins, A. (2020, July 15). *Should I forgive my narcissistic mother?* Amanda Robins Psychotherapy. https://www.amandarobinspsy chotherapy.com.au/articles/narcissistic-mother-forgiveness

Robinson, K. M. (n.d.). *Narcissists: What to do if your mother is a narcissist.* WebMD. https://www.webmd.com/mental-health/features/narcis sistic-mother

Saeed, K. (2014, July 12). *Self-forgiveness after narcissistic abuse.* Kim Saeed. https://kimsaeed.com/2014/07/11/self-forgiveness-after-narcissistic-abuse/

Saxena, S. (2022). *16 phrases to disarm a narcissist.* Choosing Therapy. https://www.choosingtherapy.com/phrases-to-disarm-a-narcissist/

Schwartz, A. (n.d.). *The narcissist versus the narcissistic personality disorder.* MentalHelp.net. https://www.mentalhelp.net/blogs/the-narcissist-versus-the-narcissistic-personality-disorder/#:~:text=It

Smith, M., & Robinson, L. (2022). *Narcissistic personality disorder.* Help-Guide. https://www.helpguide.org/articles/mental-disorders/narcissistic-personality-disorder.htm#:~:text=But%20in%20psycho logical%20terms%2C%20narcissism

Steber, C. (2017). *13 strategies for handling a toxic mom, according to experts.* Bustle. https://www.bustle.com/wellness/grown-ass-strate gies-for-handling-your-mom-if-shes-toxic

Stines, S. (2016, November 16). *How to heal from the narcissistic abuse of a parent.* GoodTherapy Therapy Blog. https://www.goodtherapy.org/blog/how-to-heal-from-narcissistic-abuse-of-parent-1116165

Streep, P. (2019). *8 things that toxic mothers have in common.* Psychology Today. https://www.psychologytoday.com/au/blog/tech-support/201905/8-things-toxic-mothers-have-in-common

Team Growth Lodge. (2022, April 25). *8 strong signs someone has quiet confidence.* Growth Lodge. https://www.growthlodge.com/8-strong-signs-someone-has-quiet-confidence/

Team Scary Mommy. (2021). *Use these 30+ phrases to disarm a narcissist when you can't avoid them.* Scary Mommy. https://www.scary mommy.com/phrases-disarm-narcissist

Villines, Z. (2022, September 12). *Grey rock method: What it is and how to use it effectively.* Medical News Today. https://www.medicalnewsto day.com/articles/grey-rock#risks

Waters, S. (2022). *Improve your confidence: 10 ways to overcome insecurities.* BetterUp. https://www.betterup.com/blog/how-to-overcome-insecurities

Whitbourne, S. K. (2021). *Why narcissists need you to doubt yourself.* Psychology Today. https://www.psychologytoday.com/au/blog/fulfillment-any-age/201508/why-narcissists-need-you-doubt-yourself

IMAGE REFERENCES

Adderley, C. (2018). *Train track surrounded by trees* [Image]. In Pexels. https://www.pexels.com/photo/train-track-surrounded-by-trees-1557688/

Bronzini, E. (2020a). *Rocky cliff beside body of water* [Image]. In Pexels. https://www.pexels.com/photo/rocky-cliff-beside-body-of-water-6161774/

Bronzini, E. (2020b). *White and black 2 print* [Image]. In Pexels. https://www.pexels.com/photo/white-and-black-2-print-5941591/

Ehlers, M. (2020). *Text on gray background* [Image]. In Pexels. https://www.pexels.com/photo/sign-texture-abstract-vintage-4116540/

Lach, R. (2021). *Man in blue crew neck t-shirt and blue denim jeans sitting on chair* [Image]. In Pexels. https://www.pexels.com/photo/man-people-woman-sitting-9464624/

Olga. (2018). *Woman in yellow dress standing on pink petaled flower field* [Image]. In Pexels. https://www.pexels.com/photo/woman-in-yellow-dress-standing-on-pink-petaled-flower-field-1146242/

Piacquadio, A. (2020). *Daughter explaining elderly mother how using smartphone* [Image]. In Pexels. https://www.pexels.com/photo/daughter-explaining-elderly-mother-how-using-smartphone-3791666/

Pixabay. (2016a). *Brown and white bear plush toy* [Image]. In Pexels. https://www.pexels.com/photo/brown-and-white-bear-plush-toy-42230/

Pixabay. (2016b). *Woman sitting on rock* [Image]. In Pexels. https://www.pexels.com/photo/adult-beach-black-dress-daylight-220452/

Pixabay. (2017). *Green tree* [Image]. In Pexels. https://www.pexels.com/photo/green-tree-268533/

Podrez, A. (2021). *Mother and daughter reading a book together* [Image]. In Pexels. https://www.pexels.com/photo/mother-and-daughter-reading-a-book-together-7505067/

RODNAE Productions. (2021). *Broken photo* [Image]. In Pexels. https://www.pexels.com/photo/fashion-love-people-woman-6670066/

Snapwire. (n.d.). *Silhouette of man raising his hands* [Image]. In Pexels. https://www.pexels.com/photo/achievement-confident-free-freedom-6945/

Studio, C. (2020). *Man in black suit jacket using smartphone* [Image]. In Pexels. https://www.pexels.com/photo/man-in-black-suit-jacket-using-smartphone-4098228/

Summers, L. (2021). *Angry black woman screaming at upset female* [Image]. In Pexels. https://www.pexels.com/photo/angry-black-woman-screaming-at-upset-female-6382698/

Turkmani, M. (2022). *Silhouette girl feeling freedom* [Image]. In Pexels. https://www.pexels.com/photo/silhouette-girl-feeling-freedom-14054281/

Vaitkevich, N. (2020). *A woman leaning on her mother* [Image]. In Pexels. https://www.pexels.com/photo/a-woman-leaning-on-her-mother-4641946/

Wellnesscenter, O. (2016). *Man and woman sitting on sidewalk* [Image]. In Pexels. https://www.pexels.com/photo/man-and-woman-sitting-on-sidewalk-226166/

Zimmerman, P. (2020). *Person writing on white paper* [Image]. In Pexels. https://www.pexels.com/photo/person-writing-on-white-paper-3746948/

Made in the USA
Monee, IL
29 May 2023

34891227R00101